THE LAKELAND MUSEUM GUIDE

Bruce Bennison

Ellenbank
Press

PARKEND HOUSE

· EDMUND BLOOD ·

NOW THE HELENA THOMPSON MUSEUM · WORKINGTON ·

For my mother and father

Time present and time past
Are both perhaps present in time future,
And time future contained in time past.

From *Four Quartets* by T. S. Eliot

Published by Ellenbank Press
The Lathes
Selby Terrace
Maryport
Cumbria CA15 6LX

First published 1991

Designed by Mary Blood

Typeset in 12pt Galliard by Butler & Tanner Ltd, Frome
Printed and bound in Great Britain
by Biddles Ltd, Guildford and King's Lynn

Cover printed by Belmont Press, Northampton

British Library Cataloguing in Publication Data
Bennison, Bruce
   The Lakeland museum guide.
   1. Museums   2. Cumbria (England)
   I. Title
   069.094278

ISBN 1–873551–02–9

Contents

Acknowledgements 6

Introduction 7

Map and Key to Museum Locations 12

The Museums

1 Carlisle and the Borders **14**

2 Whitehaven and the West Coast **37**

3 Keswick and the Lakes **65**

4 Penrith and the Pennines **97**

5 Barrow and South-West Cumbria **120**

6 Kendal and North Lancashire **138**

List of Museums by Subject Heading **159**

Acknowledgements

In compiling these descriptions I have relied heavily on the many staff, owners and volunteers associated with the museums. Theirs is a difficult task, juggling limited resources with the demands of collections that need continual care. My particular thanks to the following for permission to use illustrative material: Tony Nuttall (Solway Aviation Museum); Colonel Ralph May (Border Regiment Museum); John Hamshere (Helena Thompson Museum); Harry Fancy (Whitehaven Museum); Ranald Coyne (Muncaster Mill); Peter Nelson (Cars of the Stars); G. H. Brooks (Rydal Mount); Bruce Hanson (Brantwood); D. J. Newbegin (Killhope Wheel Lead Mining Centre); Terry Crellin (Cumbria Police Museum); Judith Clarke (Penrith Town Museum); Victoria Slowe (Abbot Hall Gallery and Museum of Lakeland Life and Industry); T. A. Schofield (Levens Hall); N. T. Stobbs (Heron Corn Mill); Dr A. J. White (Lancaster City Museum). The illustration for Birdoswald Roman Fort is from J. C. Bruce, *Handbook to the Roman Wall*, 1863; the illustration for the Caldbeck Mining Museum is from W. G. Collingwood, *Elizabethan Keswick*, republished in facsimile by Michael Moon, 1987. The drawing of the Beatrix Potter Gallery is reproduced with permission from the artist, G. R. Haybittle. Special thanks to Edmund Blood for his drawing of the Helena Thompson Museum which forms the book's frontispiece.

Author's Note: The descriptions in this Guide are entirely personal and do not reflect the opinion or policy of any public body. I have tried to ensure that the information in the Guide is as up to date as possible but, inevitably, there will be changes at some of the museums after the book goes to press. If you find changes that you feel should be included in the next edition then the publishers will be very pleased to hear from you.

Introduction

Cumbria is best known for its stunning scenery, its poets and, perhaps, for its sausages. Visitors to the region, one of the most popular holiday destinations in the British Isles, tend to spend most of their time striding across the fells or finding some means of entertainment on, or in, one of the many lakes. Many people, however, miss out on another dimension of Cumbria – the history and heritage of the County as expressed through the achievements of its people and the diversity of its environment.

The guardians of that rich heritage are the many museums and historic houses, some of which contain collections of national importance. Where else in the country can you find poetry, steam yachts, a world wildlife gallery, a museum full of pencils and an exhibition about nuclear waste reprocessing, all within a few miles of each other?

The museums of today are very different from the mausoleums of the past. A visit to Tullie House in Carlisle, for example, will provide ample proof of the progress that has been made in museum presentation. But if the museums have changed, then perhaps the visitors have too. We arrive on the steps of a museum today with a background knowledge of many subjects, often absorbed from the mass media. However a little knowledge is a dangerous thing and we need to guard against simplistic interpretations of the past that merely suit current fashions.

The role of a true museum is to collect, conserve and interpret real objects for the benefit of the community it serves, whether that community be local or national. Although museums may not appear to offer direct economic or social benefits, the simple truth is that without nurturing and maintaining them we are in danger of losing our past. And a society that loses sight of its past may well pay the price in the future by failing to learn the lessons of history.

Using the Guide

The Guide is divided into six sections, and the map on p. 12 shows the whole County with these divisions marked upon it. The museums located in each division are listed with the map under the relevant division heading. The pattern is reflected in the layout of the Guide, each section beginning with an enlarged portion of the map with the museums marked on it.

The entry for each museum begins with basic information about opening times, address, telephone number, and whether or not there is an admission charge. The other sections may require some explanation and they are listed below:

Suitability for children This is a tricky one, as my judgements are obviously subjective. Nevertheless, to make the Guide more helpful to families, I've indicated which museums I think will have limited interest for young children, and which are likely to appeal to all ages.

Refreshments This section indicates which museums have their own café or restaurant, or suggests where the visitor might find the nearest alternative eating place.

Interest The main subject areas covered by the museum are listed here. For those who wish to pursue a particular range of interests all the museums are listed by subject heading on p. 159.

How to get there This section gives directions to the museum from the nearest main road, suggests where you might park, and gives details of the nearest rail and bus stations, where relevant.

Other attractions nearby To help you plan a longer outing, I have suggested some other possibilities within easy reach. Those included in the Guide have the page numbers marked.

Getting around

Because Cumbria is such a large county, prior planning of journeys is essential – and also enjoyable. You can use the section maps as the basis for a tour of the museums in a particular area. Or you may wish to follow up a special interest by looking at the subject list on p. 159. If you plan to travel some distance to see a specific museum then do remember that it is always worth phoning first to check opening times and admission prices. Opening hours are particularly subject to variation.

By car

In general, access into, and through, the County from north to south is best achieved by using the M6 motorway. You can leave this by a number of different junctions in Cumbria. For Kendal and the South Lakes, turn off at Junction 36; for Penrith and Keswick use Junction 40; for Carlisle and the northern fringe use Junction 42/43.

Parking can be a problem. Some museums have excellent car parks but many rely on your finding public or street parking. In some areas you will need a disc to display your time of arrival. If you don't have one then go to a Tourist Information Centre or find a traffic warden.

All things considered, you may well prefer to use public transport, thus avoiding the holiday season traffic jams and lengthy searches for parking. In addition, all the family will get to see the scenery, and you will be causing less pollution.

By bus

There are an increasing number of bus companies serving Cumbria: some just cover very local routes; others are regional. The best sources of information on public transport, particularly buses, are the Tourist Information Offices and the special Cumbria Connections telephone enquiry service operated by Cumbria County Council.

The main Cumberland Motor Service (CMS) office is at: PO Box 17, Tangier Street, Whitehaven, Cumbria CA28 7XF.

For CMS enquiries phone:
Whitehaven (0946) 63222, Carlisle (0228) 48484, Workington (0900) 603080, Barrow (0229) 821325 or Kendal (0539) 722143.

National Express (Carlisle Bus Station): (0228) 48484.

Cumbrian Connections: (0228) 812812.

By train

You can hop on and off some of the London to Glasgow express trains at Lancaster, Oxenholme, Penrith or Carlisle. However some expresses do not stop at Penrith or Oxenholme, so check first – or you could end up in Crewe!

The Cumbrian Coast Line runs around the West Coast through some spectacular scenery and will take you to Barrow, Millom, Ravenglass, Whitehaven and Workington, as well as halts in between.

The much-loved Settle to Carlisle line runs through some of the most stunning northern Pennine scenery. From its remote stations you can plan circular walks up on the fells or visit market towns such as Appleby.

There are a number of good bus connections to stations on this line – look out for the publicity leaflets at Tourist Information Centres or telephone Cumbria Connections on (0228) 812812. The line also hosts regular steam specials throughout the year (check with the specialist press for details).

Finally, there is the British Rail branch line which reaches almost into the centre of the Lakes, from Oxenholme to Windermere (journey time about 20 minutes).

For information on British Rail trains, phone:
Carlisle (0228) 44711, Oxenholme (0539) 720397, Workington (0900) 602575, Whitehaven (0946) 692414, or Tourist Information Centres.

There are also three preserved steam railways in Cumbria: the Ravenglass and Eskdale Railway from Ravenglass to Dalegarth; the Lakeside and Haverthwaite Railway which terminates at its northern end on the shores of Lake Windermere; and the delightful and relatively new narrow gauge South Tynedale Railway from Alston to . . . (Well, it's getting further each year!)

Ravenglass and Eskdale Railway: (0229) 717171
Lakeside and Haverthwaite Railway (05395) 31594
South Tynedale Railway: (0434) 381696

By boat

There are ferries and launches on Windermere, Ullswater, Coniston (which has the steam yacht *Gondola*), and Derwent Water. Windermere has a car ferry linking Bowness to Far Sawrey and is a relatively quick way (depending on the season) to get over to Hawkshead from Bowness.

Ullswater Navigation and Transit Company: (0539) 721626
Windermere Iron Steamboat Company: (05395) 31188
Steam Yacht *Gondola*: (05394) 41288

Access for the disabled

Sadly, many public buildings still have serious limitations as regards access for the disabled. I am not going to point out good or bad examples because the situation may change after going to press. If you have doubts about the facilities at a particular museum then phone first – you should find the staff helpful and willing. Please bear in mind that many museums inhabit buildings designed for a totally different purpose. If you have any suggestions about access after your visit then do let the staff know.

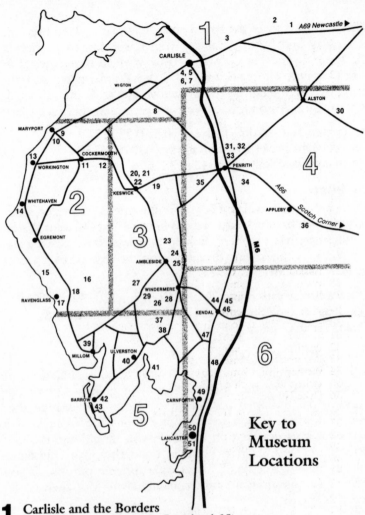

Key to
Museum
Locations

1 **Carlisle and the Borders**
  1 Roman Army Museum, Greenhead *15*
  2 Birdoswald Roman Fort, Brampton *18*
  3 Solway Aviation Museum, Carlisle Airport *21*
  4 Border Regiment Museum, Carlisle Castle *24*
  5 Carlisle Cathedral Treasury *27*
  6 Guildhall Museum, Carlisle *30*
  7 Tullie House, Carlisle *32*
  8 Caldbeck Mining Museum *35*

2 **Whitehaven and the West Coast**
   9 Senhouse Roman Army Museum, Maryport *38*
  10 Maryport Maritime Museum *41*
  11 Cumberland Toy and Model Museum, Cockermouth *44*
  12 Wythop Mill, Embleton *47*
  13 Helena Thompson Museum, Workington *50*
  14 Whitehaven Museum *53*
  15 Sellafield Visitor Centre, Seascale *56*
  16 Eskdale Corn Mill, Boot *58*
  17 Ravenglass and Eskdale Railway Museum *61*
  18 Muncaster Mill, Ravenglass *63*

3 **Keswick and the Lakes**
  19 Museum of Lakeland Mines and Quarries, Threlkeld *66*
  20 Cumberland Pencil Museum, Keswick *68*
  21 Keswick Museum and Art Gallery *71*
  22 Cars of the Stars, Keswick *74*
  23 Wordsworth Museum and Dove Cottage, Grasmere *77*
  24 Rydal Mount, Ambleside *80*
  25 Armitt Library and Museum, Ambleside *83*
  26 Beatrix Potter Gallery, Hawkshead *85*
  27 Ruskin Museum, Coniston *88*
  28 Windermere Steamboat Museum *91*
  29 Brantwood, Coniston *94*

4 **Penrith and the Pennines**
  30 Killhope Wheel Lead Mining Centre, Stanhope *98*
  31 Cumbria Police Museum, Penrith *101*
  32 Penrith Town Museum *104*
  33 Penrith Steam Museum *107*
  34 Wetheriggs Country Pottery, Penrith *111*
  35 Dalemain, Penrith *114*
  36 Dyke Nook Farm, Appleby *117*

5 **Barrow and South-West Cumbria**
  37 Stott Park Bobbin Mill, Finsthwaite *121*
  38 Lakeside and Haverthwaite Railway *123*
  39 Millom Folk Museum *125*
  40 Laurel and Hardy Museum, Ulverston *128*
  41 Lakeland Motor Museum, Holker Hall *130*
  42 Furness Museum, Barrow-in-Furness *134*
  43 The Dock, Barrow-in-Furness *136*

6 **Kendal and North Lancashire**
  44 Abbot Hall Art Gallery and Museum, Kendal *139*
  45 Museum of Lakeland Life and Industry, Kendal *142*
  46 Kendal Museum of Archaeology and Natural History *145*
  47 Levens Hall Steam Collection *148*
  48 Heron Corn Mill, Beetham *150*
  49 Steamtown Railway Museum, Carnforth *152*
  50 Lancaster City Museum *155*
  51 Lancaster Maritime Museum *157*

Carlisle and the Borders

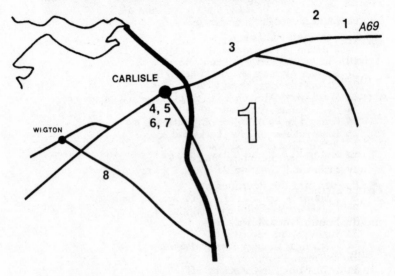

1 Roman Army Museum, Greenhead *15*
2 Birdoswald Roman Fort, Brampton *18*
3 Solway Aviation Museum, Carlisle Airport *21*
4 Border Regiment Museum, Carlisle Castle *24*
5 Carlisle Cathedral Treasury *27*
6 Guildhall Museum, Carlisle *30*
7 Tullie House, Carlisle *32*
8 Caldbeck Mining Museum *35*

Roman Army Museum
Greenhead

Open February–November *Admission charge*

Hours March–October 10.00–about 5.00, every day
February and November: 10.00–4.00, weekends only

Address Roman Army Museum, Greenhead, Northumberland

Telephone (0697) 747485

Suitability for children All ages.

Refreshments There is a tea room at the museum.

Interest Roman Army history, Hadrian's Wall.

How to get there Leave the A69 at Greenhead (east of Brampton),
go east on the B6318 and follow signs to the museum. The nearest
railway station is at Haltwhistle, but it's a long walk!

Other attractions nearby Miles of excellent walking along
Hadrian's Wall, Birdoswald Roman Fort (p. 18) and Housesteads,
and the South Tynedale Railway at Alston.

Lying outside Cumbria (but only just), the Roman Army
Museum has been included as much for its charm as anything
else. Located amongst some of the finest surviving stretches of
Hadrian's Wall, the site is adjacent to Magna, one of the Roman
Wall forts. This remarkable museum is devoted to the Roman
soldier and his life on duty here on the northern frontier of the
Empire.

At first sight the buildings containing the museum seem
relatively small. However, to the left of the shop and café is a
ramp leading down to an extensive display area. The first space
we come to is dominated by a lifesize model of a Roman
Auxiliary Cavalry Officer on horseback. (His chainmail tunic
weighs an amazing 35 lb!) Around the walls are colourful shields
painted in the Roman manner, as well as a number of display
cases containing a wide variety of objects relating to the soldiers'

everyday life. Food and cooking are featured – oyster shells, pottery and a modern version of an original Roman cookery book – as well as craft-working tools, and various iron and bronze fittings. There is also an interesting display of preserved leatherwork, with boots and sandals serving to illustrate the sophisticated Roman approach to protecting the feet – 'trench foot' was probably rife in the chilly bogs of northern Britain 2000 years ago.

On one side of the room is a large model of the nearby fort with a press-button audio commentary; on the other side is a gallery with another audio-visual display, though the visual is fairly static. There are also some interpretative panels featuring some of the many sites along the Wall, from Birdoswald to South Shields, as well as models of a typical headquarters building and of a granary (similar to that which can be seen at Birdoswald). More ramps and steps lead to a lower level which houses a large video theatre where you can see a programme about the site. In this same area are some full-sized reconstructions of a barrack block room and a scene including an elaborate working Roman baggage wagon. Don't miss the large aerial colour photographs of Vindolanda, Housesteads and Chesters which provide intriguing insights into the design and location of these Roman forts.

In the next room suits of Roman armour are proudly presented on stands, each style having a curious Latin name such as Lorica Segmentata and Lorica Cuirass. Weapons line the walls and large artists' reconstructions give us a glimpse of what life must have been like in the forts. As you leave this room, look at the carefully produced wall charts displaying the history of each of the known Roman legions. If you look closely you will see that every now and then one is listed as destroyed – what awful tragedy lies behind that simple statement?

Even though these events took place nearly 2,000 years ago, this museum seems to succeed in bringing the Roman Army to life, perhaps because it bears a distinct resemblance to a modern military museum. Do not expect too much in the way of genuine Roman objects here; the emphasis is on replicas and reconstructions. Nevertheless the result has a vividness and immediacy which fires the imagination; maybe it's the tomb-like atmosphere of the basement setting that does it!

The Roman Army Museum provides a good introduction to the complex organisation of the Roman Army and succeeds in putting flesh on the dry historical bones of that great monument, Hadrian's Wall.

Birdoswald Roman Fort
Brampton

Open Easter–October, and at other times by arrangement
Admission charge

Hours 9.30–5.30, every day

Address Birdoswald Roman Fort, Gilsland, Brampton, Cumbria, CA6 7DD

Telephone (06977) 47602

Suitability for children All ages.

Refreshments Tea and coffee available at the museum.

Interest Roman history.

How to get there The museum is signposted from either Brampton or Greenhead on the A69 Carlisle to Newcastle road. The nearest railway station is at Brampton, a good walk away.

Other attractions nearby Roman Army Museum (p. 15), Lanercost Priory (owned by English Heritage) and the South Tynedale Railway at Alston. There is some excellent walking along Hadrian's Wall, so take your boots.

Birdoswald represents Cumbria's main contribution to the interpretation of Hadrian's Wall, apart from Tullie House in Carlisle (p. 32). Based upon an original Roman Wall fort, this fascinating centre brings together different historical elements to create a complex and intriguing site. Overlooking the Irthing Gorge, Birdoswald is located in one of the most picturesque settings along the whole Wall. The Victorian farmhouse and outbuildings are gradually being converted into a visitor centre, whilst archaeological excavations are revealing more and more of the underlying Roman fort.

Known as 'Banna' to the Romans, the story of Birdoswald is told here through a colourful series of interpretative panels inside a tastefully converted barn. Without going into a detailed history of Hadrian's Wall, suffice to say that Emperor Hadrian's grand design to separate barbarian from Roman was begun shortly after his visit to Britain in AD 120. In the following decades the Wall underwent major changes. Persistent attacks (presumably from northern tribes) resulted in the main Roman forts being moved up to the line of the barrier itself, thus facilitating military expeditions into barbarian territory. The original turf wall at Birdoswald was replaced by stone and a supply road was built to link the Wall forts. Further ditches and the *Vallum* (a sort of no-man's-land) were added to the Wall itself to create a formidable boundary at the very edge of the Roman world.

Building stone from Birdoswald Fort

Outside and beyond the farmhouse lie the remains of the fort, most of which are accessible to the visitor. The entire perimeter wall is clearly visible, and the recently excavated granaries (dating to around AD 200) have been carefully consolidated and left exposed. After walking around the site go through the south gate to the edge of the bluff, and take a few moments to look out over Irthing Gorge – the view is tremendous.

If you turn around at this point you can begin to trace the early origins of the farmhouse. It began life in the late sixteenth century as a bastle or peel house (a sort of miniature fortified tower block). The style of this early building was continued by a later owner of the farm, one Henry Norman, a true Victorian Romantic and an enthusiastic archaeologist. He created the Birdoswald we see today, extending the farm, rebuilding the tower, and carrying out the excavations on the fort walls and gates. Birdoswald's later history, after the main Roman period, is one of the most interesting of all the Wall forts and there are some intriguing signs that the site may have been re-used in the late fourth century by somebody of noble status.

Birdoswald is well supplied with facilities for the visitor – a good car park, toilets and a shop. It is quieter than some of the other Wall sites and is well worth a visit for that reason alone (now there's a statement with built-in obsolescence!). Whilst you are at the site take a walk down to Harrow's Scar milefort, a few hundred yards to the east.

If you visit the site on a weekday you are likely to be treated to the spectacular but noisy low-flying jets heading for the nearby RAF range at Spadeadam, and if you watch carefully you can occasionally see small rockets being fired at the planes to give the pilots a more realistic combat environment.

Birdoswald is a fascinating site, straddling the lush green vale to the south and the high open moors to the north. It is a place where you can almost breathe in the history, and gain a sense of its continuity from Roman times through to the present day.

Solway Aviation Museum
Carlisle Airport

Open Easter–September *Admission charge*

Hours 2.00–4.00, Sundays only

Address Solway Aviation Museum, Carlisle Airport, Crosby on Eden, Carlisle, Cumbria

Telephone No phone at time of writing

Suitability for children 10 years and above.

Refreshments Available in airport building.

Interest Aviation history, military history.

How to get there The airport is west of Brampton on the B6264, and signposted off this road. There is no easy access by public transport.

Other attractions nearby Tullie House (p. 32), Birdoswald Roman Fort (p. 18) and the Roman Army Museum (p. 15).

This is a surprise indeed, an opportunity to climb inside the cockpit of a Vulcan bomber, and in Cumbria too! During the Second World War places such as Carlisle, Kirkbride, Longtown, Kingston and Annan were all used at one time or another for training, maintenance or storage. Carlisle Airport also had a wartime role and, of all the local contenders, has survived as the city's airport and the setting for the Solway Aviation Society's collection of historic aircraft.

The most prominent of the four planes on display by the main airport building is the Vulcan bomber, best known of the so-called 'V Bomber' force that spearheaded Britain's nuclear deterrent in the 1960s. In the cramped cockpit only the pilot and co-pilot (of the five-man crew) had the luxury of ejector seats, and discreetly tucked away 'bladder bags' took the place of a WC. The Vulcan on display, XJ 823, was the standby aircraft on Operation Black Buck during the Falklands War. Stepping up inside the cockpit is a remarkable experience rarely open to us civilians, and a tape recording of the plane in flight makes you feel that you are flying it yourself!

Vulcan bomber

The other aircraft on display are an English Electric Canberra bomber, T4 WE188, and a Gloster Meteor, WS 832. Both these planes represent firsts in aviation design: the Meteor was the first jet fighter (and the only such Allied fighter to see action in the Second World War); the Canberra was Britain's first jet bomber, making its maiden flight in 1949. At the time of writing the Society members are also restoring a Lightning Interceptor. (The Ministry of Defence had insisted that the wings be cut off and glued back to prevent enthusiasts attempting to fly it again!)

A small display cabin houses informative displays on local airfield history as well as aviation memorabilia and instruments from various historic aircraft. The collection includes a radar set from a Lancaster bomber and an astrograph (used for navigation) from a Flying Fortress. There is also a well-preserved instrument panel from a Miles Magister that a certain L. A. C. Senior carelessly crashed into Ullswater in December 1940. He survived the experience, but no doubt learned to his cost how cold a Cumbrian lake in mid-winter can be. The panel was recovered by divers in 1974.

Perhaps the most interesting display is the one recounting the story of nearby Spadeadam. The low-flying RAF jets which have caused such controversy in the Lake District are often on their way to RAF Spadeadam, north-east of Brampton, but 30 years ago this wild area of moorland played a very different role. In 1955 Britain agreed to take part in the development of an intermediate ballistic missile called Blue Streak, intended as part of the UK nuclear deterrent. By 1960 it had been declared obsolete, but development continued on the rocket as a satellite launcher instead. Whilst the rocket was actually built in Stevenage, it was tested at Spadeadam, partly for security reasons but mainly because so few people live in the area.

The tests at Spadeadam were as close as the scientists could get to launch conditions, with only four bolts holding the rocket in place on the ground. (If the bolts had not held, Cumbria might have been the first English county to enter the space race!) The project ended in 1971 when Britain was persuaded to join the space shuttle programme, instead of continuing with its own contribution to a European satellite launcher. The display at the museum includes many interesting photographs of the rocket and the technology used.

The Solway Aviation Museum exists thanks to a small band of enthusiasts who, rather like steam buffs, strive to preserve large and complex bits of machinery, often with minimal resources but unlimited devotion. You will not find anything like these aircraft anywhere else in Cumbria. And if you're lucky a novice pilot from the local flying school may even provide free aerial entertainment during your visit.

Border Regiment Museum
Carlisle Castle

Open All year, all week *Admission free, but you need to pay to get into the castle*

Hours April–September: Monday–Saturday 9.30–6.00, Sunday 10.00–6.00

October–April: Monday–Saturday 9.30–4.00, Sunday 10.00–4.00

Address Queen Mary's Tower, The Castle, Carlisle, Cumbria CA3 8UR

Telephone (0228) 32774

Suitability for children 10 years and above.

Refreshments Available in nearby Tullie House café.

Interest Military history.

How to get there The museum is inside Carlisle Castle which is close to Tullie House Museum and can be seen from outside the cathedral.

Other attractions nearby The Castle, Tullie House Museum (p. 32), Guildhall Museum (p. 30) and Carlisle Cathedral Treasury (p. 27).

The Border Regiment Museum (known in full as the Border Regiment and King's Own Royal Border Regiment Museum) is devoted to the history of Cumbria's local regiments. Its guidebook asks: 'Have you ever wondered how Britain's Empire was won and run by the smallest army of any major power of the time?' If so, here is the place to search for answers.

Opened in 1932 and originally housed in the adjacent Keep, the museum moved to its present home in 1973. The exhibits are set out on two floors and you will need to bypass the shop to start upstairs. The display cases are laid out in chronological order, and some of the most colourful and interesting items come from the eighteenth and nineteenth centuries.

In Case One look for the medal commemorating the notorious Duke of Cumberland's capture of Carlisle Castle from the forces of the Young Pretender in December 1745. There is also a fragment of the Colours of the 2nd Battalion 34th Regiment in Case Two, given by Ensign Moyle Sherer who was taken prisoner following a battle at Maya Pass in the Pyrenees during the Peninsular War. Sherer wrote of his capture: 'the worst feature of the whole affair was that Boult [the French commander] kissed me before all his staff and called me a brave man'.

Also in this case are the curved sword and soldier's jacket belonging to Ensign John Bell of the Royal Westmorland Regiment. In 1814 his mother took him by coach from Appleby to Portsmouth to join the fleet sailing for south-west France. Unfortunately the fleet had already sailed but on hearing that it was becalmed off the Isle of Wight they hired a boat and joined it there. The vagaries of the British weather caught up with Mrs Bell however; she was stuck on board ship and had to sail with the Regiment to France. Ensign Bell must be one of the few soldiers ever to have taken their mother to war with them!

Colour and curiosity are the main characteristics of the displays from these early years. Chinese dragon standards, drums and relics of the Boer Wars are just a few examples of the unusual items you will find. The relics of the two World Wars, however, will mean the most to many visitors. There are many poignant stories recorded from both conflicts and it is worth taking time to read the labels and study the objects. One wonders, for example, what ever happened to W. Wood after his shaving mirror was so dramatically pierced by shrapnel. Did he live to tell the tale? On day one of the Battle of the Somme, 1 July 1916, the 11th Battalion of the Border Regiment was amongst the first wave 'over the top'. Twenty-five officers and 800 men went into action, a few tragic minutes of carnage left just three officers and 300 men alive. The counties of Cumberland and Westmorland took a long time to recover from their grievous loss. During the Second World War all the battalions of the Regiment played their part, the 1st Battalion becoming part of the 1st Air Landing Brigade who saw action at Arnhem, the 'bridge too far'.

More recent conflicts, such as those in the Cameroons, Aden, Cyprus and Northern Ireland, are represented by displays covering the amalgamated King's Own Royal Border Regiment. It is a sad fact of late twentieth-century life that terrorism occupies a great deal of the British Army's time. Accordingly, the displays include those symbols of the Northern Ireland conflict, the Armalite and the rubber bullet.

Like many museums devoted to military history, the Border Regiment Museum is a shrine to the men who, over the years, have soldiered for their County. You will need patience and understanding to reap the benefits from these displays but there are fascinating stories to be learnt here for those who care to read and look.

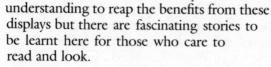

Drummer of the
34th Cumberland Regiment,
1753

Cathedral Treasury
Carlisle

Open All year *Admission charge*

Hours Normal opening hours of the Cathedral (best to try from 10.00–5.00)

Address Carlisle Cathedral, Castle Street, Carlisle, Cumbria

Telephone (0228) 35169

Suitability for children 10 years and above.

Refreshments Available nearby in the Buttery, opposite the main entrance to the Cathedral.

Interest Church history, embroidery and metalwork.

How to get there The Cathedral is located close to Tullie House and the Castle. There are pay and display car parks on West Walls and Devonshire Walk. Carlisle railway station and the bus station are both about 10 minutes walk away.

Other attractions nearby The Guildhall Museum (p. 30), Tullie House (p. 32), Border Regiment Museum (p. 24), and the Castle. Also the Carlisle Visitor Centre and Tourist Information in the old market building in the Greenmarket.

Carlisle Cathedral Treasury is a new development in a building that dates back to 1096 and the reign of King William Rufus. You will find the Treasury in a superbly built underground gallery, where a short passageway leads into the main area. On the wall of the passage is displayed a blue cope made of Italian damask silk and embroidered with silk and metal threads. It is of English origin and dates to around 1440. Some sections of it, in particular the border, are even earlier.

Inside the main gallery there is a series of wall charts and display cases. The wall charts tell the story of Christian Cumbria, beginning with the Roman period and moving on through the lives of some of the local saints. St Kentigern (or St Mungo, as he is known in Scotland) was the Bishop of Glasgow in AD 550. There are eight churches dedicated to him in the Diocese of Carlisle and these are marked on one of a series of useful maps in the room. St Cuthbert visited Carlisle several times, the last visit taking place in AD 686. His life is featured in the fine paintings to be found on the back of the choir stalls in the Cathedral. The story of early Christianity continues with a section on the Celtic crosses – the best examples in Cumbria are perhaps those at Bewcastle and Gosforth.

The origins of the Cathedral are covered in the section on Norman history, and there is also a display of Viking objects unearthed during the excavations for the Treasury gallery. They give some tantalising clues to the everyday life of the Norse settlers in Carlisle. The site was in fact a cemetery on which over 40 graves have been discovered, many yielding objects such as the 'Sceat' and 'Styca' coins shown here. There are also some clothing hooks made of brass and silver, and some ornate tenth-century copper belt fittings. The most interesting item is probably the superb thirteenth-century jet crucifix.

The central display cases hold the historic plate belonging to the Cathedral and surrounding churches. The first display contains the Cathedral's own plate and – believe it or not – a pair of walrus tusks! There is also a Holy Water basin, or Stoop, from St Mary's in Wreay, a village nearby. The second display shows the original charter of 1542, establishing the Dean and Chapter for the Cathedral. The next case is full of plate from local Diocesan churches and includes Bishop Samuel Waldegrave's Verge (a silver staff) dating to 1866.

Dean Tait, who was Dean of the Cathedral from 1850 to 1856, later went on to become Archbishop of Canterbury. Here, in another display case, are his handwritten instructions for his memorial window, some prayer books and an amusing cartoon drawing done for his daughters with the motto 'Be a good Tait'!

In one corner of the gallery is a more recent cope, which formerly belonged to Bishop Henry Williams (1920–46). It is a colourful piece of goldwork upon a bright red cloth; displayed with it are his mitre and pastoral staff. Along one wall of the room are two large wooden chests, one containing fragments of the restored Broughton Triptych (which can be seen in the main body of the building), and the other whose main claim to fame appears to be its huge locks.

A collection of modern limited edition plate commissioned for many of the English cathedrals forms the final display of metalwork.

The Treasury is a new and interesting addition to the museums of Cumbria. You will not find another display of this sort anywhere in the County so it's well worth a visit. The Cathedral itself is, of course, a superb building with a wealth of history in its own right. Why not visit all three attractions – the Castle, Tullie House and the Cathedral – and make a day of it?

The Guildhall Museum
Carlisle

Open All year *Admission free*

Hours Tuesday–Saturday (and Bank Holidays) 11.00–4.00; Sunday 12.00–5.00

Address The Guildhall Museum, Greenmarket, Carlisle, Cumbria

Telephone (0228) 34781

Suitability for children 10 years and above.

Refreshments There is a restaurant on the ground floor of the museum building.

Interest Local and guild history.

How to get there The Guildhall is located in central Carlisle near the Tourist Information Office and the Visitor Centre. Carlisle is just off the M6 at Junction 42/43. There are good rail connections and the main bus and railway stations are about 10 minutes walk away.

Other attractions nearby Tullie House (p. 32), Border Regiment Museum and Castle (p. 24), and Carlisle Cathedral Treasury (p. 27).

The Guildhall is one of the earliest surviving buildings in the city of Carlisle. It was originally the home of Richard and Alice Redeness who had a house built on the site in 1407 and lived there for the rest of their lives. Richard Redeness was an important member of the local community and he left his house to the city in his will. After his death it was quickly put to use by the city's trade guilds.

 The building is timber-framed, and the infill panels between the timbers are tile-brick on the outside walls and 'wattle and daub' on the internal walls. This type of construction, though common further south, is rare in Cumbria. The Guildhall was most recently renovated in 1979 and then reopened as a museum devoted to guild history and the city of Carlisle.

You first climb a flight of stairs up to a small shop and various displays including one about the old city gates (which boasted the largest padlocks I have ever seen!). There are also some stocks from Market Place (last used to punish a wrongdoer in 1827), and silver owned by the various trade guilds.

Off this main display gallery is the Shoemakers' Room, still used by the Guild of Shoemakers for their meetings. The room contains various items pertaining to their trade, including a statue of St Crispin, the patron saint of shoemakers.

Up another flight of stairs is the Tanners' Room which curiously contains the Weavers' Guild Banner and a rustic elm chair dated 1644. In a case in the middle of the room is a copy of the huge gold mace of the city; the original is still in use today.

The Weavers' Room next door is filled by a Caldbeck hand-loom once used to weave blankets and the characteristic grey cloth worn by John Peel (of 'D'ye ken' fame). The Merchants' Room has a display of cock-fighting instruments, as well as the old weights and measures of the city which were used to set fair standards for trading. The Butchers' Room has some medieval pottery including an early money box and a chamber pot. For some unknown reason this room also contains a display entitled 'Dress and Undress', with various items of ladies' underwear.

Carlisle used to have eight trade guilds and each one had a room in the Guildhall. Guild members were originally the only citizens entitled to vote, a factor which led to their exploitation by prospective MPs in the seventeenth century, and subsequently to their decline. Today only four guilds survive: the Butchers, Merchants, Shoemakers, and Skinners and Glovers.

The Guildhall is a fine building and a pleasant surprise within this city of red sandstone. As a museum featuring the early organisation of labour it is unique in Cumbria, and makes a very worthwhile stop on a day trip.

Tullie House
Carlisle

Open All year *Admission charge*

Hours October–Easter: 10.00–5.00, every day
Easter–September 10.00–7.00

Address Castle Street, Carlisle, Cumbria, CA3 8TP

Telephone (0228) 34781

Suitability for children Excellent for all ages.

Refreshments There are excellent facilities inside the museum.

Interest Romans, Border Reivers, natural history, social history, fine art, and much besides.

How to get there There are good rail connections and the main bus and rail stations are about 10 minutes walk away. 'Pay and display' car parks are situated about 5 minutes walk away, and there is a coach stop by the museum.

Other attractions nearby Guildhall Museum (p. 30), Border Regiment Museum (p. 24) and Carlisle Castle, the Lanes Shopping Centre and Carlisle Visitor Centre.

In this, perhaps the most important museum development in the North-West of England for many years, the city of Carlisle has invested in a spectacular celebration of its complex and turbulent history. The old Tullie House museum reopened in 1991, incorporating some superb new visitor-orientated features. The building had just opened when this entry was being written so apologies if some of the details have changed.

The museum is divided into two main areas. On the ground floor are comprehensive visitor facilities including a shop and large refreshment hall, educational workspace, and a lecture/film theatre available for use by outside groups. There is also a new and fully air-conditioned temporary Exhibitions Gallery for the display of contemporary visual arts.

Part of the museum is an elegant seventeenth-century town house, with Victorian additions, set in an attractive garden. The Jacobean wing includes an elegant panelled room, the original Jacobean staircase and some colourful Victorian tilework. This area is now given over to changing displays of the museum's extensive collections of fine and decorative art.

However it is perhaps upstairs in the Border Galleries that the most entertaining exhibits are to be found. Here the region's turbulent history is graphically depicted in an incredible audio-visual display that takes us through some of the livelier episodes in the history of the Reivers, those violent families who lived by the sword and subjected the area to disturbance for many years. The scene unfolds before you as the luckless warden of Carlisle Castle attempts to enforce the law against the Reivers' brand of territorial piracy – prepare to be enthralled!

The Wildlife Gallery takes you into the heart of the Cumbrian countryside. The sky above you changes from night to day and the air is filled with the sights and sounds of Cumbria, including a low-flying jet and a flight of geese! Here also is a rockface complete with birds of prey, and a mine tunnel which children will love to explore.

Roman influence in the area is well represented by a massive modelled section of the turf wall which constituted the main Cumbrian component of the Emperor Hadrian's formidable barrier across the north of England. Here you can climb up a guardhouse turret and look down on the scene below. There is even a Roman arrow-firer to be tried out – safely!

The secrets of archaeology are revealed in the worm's eye view of a Roman street in which a Roman lady has come out to fill her water jar, unaware of our presence below. Under her feet a slice through history shows the yet-to-be-discovered evidence of the ancient settlement that was to become Carlisle.

All this re-creation is suddenly interrupted by something very real. A viewing window has been cleverly placed for us to look out towards the huge bulk of Carlisle Castle. All around us are the sounds of medieval conflict (hopefully inside the museum!), and apparitions of Robert the Bruce and the heroic Warden de Harcla stand at our side.

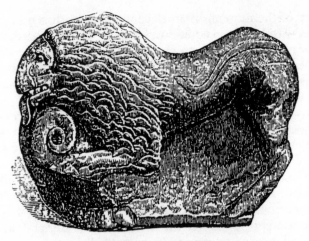
Roman lion sculpture

Later conflicts are covered too. We can peep into Isaac Tullie's study, as it might have appeared when he sat down to record in his diary how the Roundheads had laid siege to the Royalist city in 1644. The last siege in England took place in Carlisle in 1745, when the English were in pursuit of Bonnie Prince Charlie. By this time our chronicler, Isaac Tullie, had been dead for 100 years but here he is eerily brought to life again to tell us of the siege.

Carlisle's railway heritage is not forgotten either – you can sample the delights of third- or first-class carriage compartments (no unfair comparisons with BR, please). There are other displays too: social history; archaeology; and a setting from one of Carlisle's famous 'State Management' pubs. (The pubs were once nationalised here!)

Tullie House is a stunning place, incorporating some state of the art technology. It places Carlisle firmly on the map as a city proud of its past and confident of its future. Whether you are just visiting the area or you are a local resident, you cannot afford to miss this museum.

Caldbeck Mining Museum
Caldbeck

Open March–December, and at other times by arrangement
Admission charge

Hours Mid-March–October: 11.00–5.00, Tuesdays–Sundays and
Bank Holiday Mondays
November–December: 11.00–5.00, weekends only

Address Priest's Mill, Caldbeck, Cumbria, CA7 8DR

Telephone (06998) 369

Suitability for children 10 years and above.

Refreshments In the main Mill.

Interest Mining history.

How to get there Caldbeck is on the B5299 south-west of Carlisle.
There is poor public transport access.

Other attractions nearby Tullie House (p. 32). Caldbeck is a
good starting point for walks into the fells behind Skiddaw.

You enter the museum through a shop that stocks some outdoor
gear and an excellent selection of books on mining and geology.
It is worth pausing at the map of local mines as it will help you
understand the displays inside. There are numerous photographs
of the many obscure and long defunct mines which, apart from
the odd spoil heap or dark tunnel entrance, are now almost
invisible amongst the fells. Many are places that you would pass
while fell-walking. Greenside Mine near Glenridding is one,
lying beside the path up to Helvellyn; Coniston copper mines
are prominent on the side of the Old Man; and Force Crag
is still worked in Coledale, en route from Braithwaite up to
Grasmoor.

Some of the Lake District mines pioneered developments
in mining engineering. Greenside Mine, for example, had an
underground electric railway in 1890. There are all sorts of

strange items on display here – boots, candles, picks, shovels, lamps and a length of slow-burning fusewire, to name but a few. There are drill bits of all shapes and sizes – high-speed compressed air drills and larger screw thread drills (which look like unicorn horns) used for hand boring dynamite holes. You can also see two examples of 'in–out' boards with the names of the miners on them. They were used to count the men in and out in advance of any blasting and at the end of the shift.

The minerals are worth a close look. Some of the names of the specimens – sphalerite, arsenopyrite, mimetite – are as colourful as the minerals themselves. Then there is the more familiar graphite, used in the famous local pencil-making industry in Keswick.

Caldbeck Mining Museum displays over 300 years of mining history (some of the rock wedges apparently date back to the 1600s). Its display area may be small but it covers an enormous amount of history. The rest of Priest's Mill is also very interesting, and the restored eighteenth-century mill now contains a number of small shops and a tea room. If you are interested in exploring the history of Lakeland mining further, contact the museum curators for details of summer trips to surface remains in the area.

Sorting the ore in a medieval mine

Whitehaven
and the
West Coast

9   Senhouse Roman Army Museum, Maryport *38*
10 Maryport Maritime Museum *41*
11 Cumberland Toy and Model Museum, Cockermouth *44*
12 Wythop Mill, Embleton *47*
13 Helena Thompson Museum, Workington *50*
14 Whitehaven Museum *53*
15 Sellafield Visitor Centre, Seascale *56*
16 Eskdale Corn Mill, Boot *58*
17 Ravenglass and Eskdale Railway Museum *61*
18 Muncaster Mill, Ravenglass *63*

Senhouse Roman Army Museum
Maryport

Open All year *Admission charge*

Hours July–September: 10.00–5.00, every day
Restricted opening out of season–please phone for details

Address The Battery, Maryport, Cumbria CA15 6JD

Telephone (0900) 816168

Suitability for children 10 years and above.

Refreshments A café is planned for the museum, but if it is not yet open then try the sandwich bar by the harbour or the cafés on Senhouse Street.

Interest Roman army history.

How to get there Up on the clifftop north of the town, accessible by road and signposted from the town centre. Maryport railway station is about 15 minutes walk away.

Other attractions nearby Maryport Maritime Museum (p. 41), steamboats in the harbour, and Roman coastal defence remains. Superb views of the Isle of Man and Southern Scotland.

This relatively new museum houses a collection of Roman altars and sculptured stones built up over a period of 400 years by the Senhouse family. The Senhouse family, mentioned elsewhere in this Guide (p. 41) were responsible for developing the harbour and town of Maryport in the eighteenth and nineteenth centuries. Started in 1599, this is the oldest antiquarian collection in Britain. And it all comes from a single site, the Roman fort on the clifftop just behind the present museum building, built around AD 122 as part of the coastal defences that complemented Hadrian's Wall.

The Battery building in which the museum is housed was

constructed in 1884 as a Royal Naval Reserve Gun Training Centre. The building was subsequently used by the Sea Cadets up until 1980. After a serious fire the decaying building was taken over by a trust and made into the present museum.

Roman carving from Alauna, Maryport

The collection reflects the strange religious mixture of the early years of Roman Britain – the Celtic gods worshipped by the native population and the 'imported' Roman gods worshipped by the Army. (Christianity seems relatively simple by comparison!). The altars that you see in the museum were dedicated by important commanders, civilians associated with the army, and members of various units stationed at the fort. M. Maerius Agrippa – Commander of Cohort I, Hispana (from Spain) – is one example. He went on to command the British fleet and became the chief finance officer (procurator) for the province of Britain. Another of the stones was dedicated by a Greek doctor, Asclepius Aubus Egnatius, and other individuals came from the Adriatic and Belgium.

One of the most impressive features of the museum is the shrine dedicated to the Emperor Hadrian, whose statue looms out at you from the gloom. There are also reconstructions of armour worn by rather fierce-looking lifesize models. One suit, with cattle horn as its main protective material, catches the eye. It is estimated that 32 horns would have been needed to make one suit, so a whole auxiliary unit of 1,000 men would have needed 16,000 cattle to supply the material for their armour! However this is not too implausible if you consider that each suit was made to last about ten years.

As well as altars there are fragments of gravestones, and artist's impressions of the death ceremonies. These reconstruction paintings are placed strategically around the museum and bring the stones to life by placing them in their historical context. The museum also contains some Celtic carvings. The Serpent Stone, a large octagonal shaft with a Celtic head at the top and a serpent carved up one side, is the most striking. The whole stone is carved in the form of a huge phallus and probably represents fertility and rebirth after death. Another stone has a carving of a wheel incorporated into it. The wheel-god is strongly represented in stones from this area and this probably indicates a high proportion of Celtic troops in the auxiliary units stationed here.

This museum also serves to point us towards other sites to be found along the Cumbrian coast (such as the recently excavated fort at Crosscanonby Saltpans a mile to the north), where evidence can be seen of the great military strategy that lay behind the construction of Hadrian's Wall.

The Senhouse Roman Army Museum is a fascinating place to visit. Don't be put off by the fact that most of the exhibits are just rather odd-looking stones. These stones speak, so be prepared to listen! And, after listening for a while, step outside, look out over the Solway and imagine you're a Roman soldier in Emperor Hadrian's army guarding the northernmost limit of the civilised world.

Maritime Museum
Maryport

Open All year

Hours Easter–September: Monday–Saturday, 10.00–5.00 (closed for lunch 1.00–2.00 on Saturdays); Sunday, 2.00–5.00.
October–Easter: Monday–Saturday, 10.00–12.00, 2.00–4.00 (closed on Wednesday)

Address 1 Senhouse Street, Maryport, Cumbria, CA15 6AB

Telephone (0900) 813738

Suitability for children 10 years and above.

Refreshments There's a small café just across the harbour bridge.

Interest Maritime history.

How to get there Maryport railway station is about 10 minutes walk away. The museum is located by the harbour, next to the road bridge into the harbour development area. There's disc parking on the street nearby.

Other attractions nearby Senhouse Roman Army Museum (p. 38), Cumberland Toy and Model Museum (p. 44), and Helena Thompson Museum (p. 50).

The maritime history of Maryport goes right back to the Roman era – the Roman Army used the mouth of the River Ellen to shelter their supply ships whilst the large fort was being built on the nearby clifftop. The town itself dates back to 1749 when the then Lord of the Manor, Humphrey Senhouse II, was empowered by an Act of Parliament to build a new port for the coal trade, naming it after his wife Mary.

The Maritime Museum occupies three floors of the building. The ground floor is shared between the Tourist Information Centre, a model of the barque *Mary Graham,* and a history of Maryport Harbour and its ships told through old photographs. There are some paintings too, by members of Maryport's most

prominent nineteenth-century artistic family, the Mitchells. A brass plaque on the wall commemorates the lives lost in the sinking of the barque *Midas*. The last of the sailing vessels built by the Ritsons, a local shipbuilding firm, she was launched in 1896 but sank in the Pacific on her maiden voyage.

Upstairs on the first floor the main room is dominated by a model of a Watson 46-foot lifeboat, and more lifeboat memorabilia is displayed on the second floor. Thomas Ismay, a famous son of Maryport and founder of the White Star Line, has a whole display devoted to him and his ships, including menu cards, passenger lists and models.

Other items in this room include some vicious and no doubt effective boarding spikes from the Royal Navy; telescopes; a 'ditty box', used to carry the personal belongings of sailor Edward Gilbertson; and a sperm whale tooth, delicately etched with the figure of Liberty. (This type of carving or 'scrimshaw' work was a popular pastime amongst sailors.) In the central display case are some marlin spikes and various sail-making tools, while navigation is represented by a sextant, a ship's compass and some chart-making instruments.

In a side room is a display on Fletcher Christian, of mutiny on the *Bounty* fame. Christian was born near Cockermouth in

1764 and ran away to sea at the age of 16. The story of the famous mutiny is described in some detail and the exhibits include Christian's sea chest.

On the second floor are models of a Viking longship and a Roman trading vessel, as well as pottery and porcelain featuring elements from Maryport's past. A painted board commemorates people saved by the town's lifeboats over the years, and a collection of lifebelts, certificates of service and photographs illustrates the lives of their brave crews. The first lifeboat came to Maryport in 1865, but the gradual decay of the launching facilities forced the eventual closure of the station in 1950.

Many visitors to the town today are unaware of its fascinating history and long-standing shipbuilding tradition. A graphic illustration of Maryport's former life can be seen in the photographs of some of the 'broadside' launches of new ships into the River Ellen. If you step outside the museum you will see where the launches used to take place just across the river. You can imagine the noise and celebration – it must have been a fine sight indeed.

Lastly there are the preserved steamships to be found in the harbour – a former Clyde steam tug called the *Flying Buzzard* and an old Admiralty victualling lighter called *VIC 69*. Although both are currently firmly moored to the dockside and are undergoing active restoration you can still get a flavour of life at sea from a walk around their decks. The cargo hold of *VIC 69* contains a lively interpretative display about sail and steam power.

Cumberland Toy and Model Museum
Cockermouth

Open February–November *Admission charge*

Hours 10.00–5.00, every day

Address Bank's Court, Market Place, Cockermouth, Cumbria

Telephone (0900) 827606

Suitability for children All ages.

Refreshments There are several cafés close by in the town centre.

Interest Toys and model trains.

How to get there Find Main Street in the centre of town and head east to Market Place. Bank's Court is just off the street and the museum is signposted. There is pay and display parking at Market Place or in a large car park by Wakefield Road, near the river. The nearest railway station is at Maryport and buses run from there to Cockermouth, stopping in Main Street.

Other attractions nearby Wordsworth's House (owned by the National Trust). Cockermouth also has some interesting off-street courtyards with shops selling antiques and gifts.

This is definitely a place for children of all ages, including adults! Be warned however: a visit to this museum could leave you with a serious case of nostalgia. Owner and curator Rod Moore makes railway models as part of his business and you can often see him at work at his desk. For the price of a few 10 pence coins, fellow enthusiasts can try their hands at model car racing or bringing an early electric train set to life. There are also small play areas for younger children to try badge-making and other activities.

On entering the museum you see a large central display consisting of two train layouts: one of Hornby Dublo material;

the other of earlier tinplate stock. Generally speaking the displays are set out chronologically. Few people realise, perhaps, that the first electric model trains date from before 1914. Looking around the gallery you come across curiosities such as the clockwork chicken, the ingenious 'Puff Boot Paff' (which proves to be a candle-powered boat!) and the delightful Camphor Craft, a small and delicate sailing craft constructed of balsa wood and cloth, which used the properties of camphor and water surface tension to propel itself. A very different sort of ship is represented by the card model of the RMS *Queen Mary*. Layers of printed card, each with a detailed coloured plan of a deck, are sandwiched together to form a simple but instructive model of one of the finest ocean liners of its day. It is the trains that dominate however – the brightly coloured tinplate wagons and the superb finish of the locomotives, epitomised by the Hornby '0' gauge 'Princess Elizabeth' still in its box.

The displays of toys from more recent years reflect the introduction of new materials (particularly plastics) and smaller, more efficient electric motors. As electrical technology improved, model trains could be made to smaller and smaller scales; '00' gauge was introduced and the method of power pick-up changed from stud contact and three-rail to the familiar two-rail contact of today. Meccano is well represented, here, with some of its infinite construction possibilities, including machines run from external power sources such as steam, clockwork and electric. Experiments with new methods of propulsion for models include a model plane powered by carbon dioxide from a canister normally used for putting the fizz in a soda syphon.

Upstairs, the centre of the room is again occupied by a large layout – a Scalextric race track. Have a go, but you will find that you can't spin the cars off at the corners! There is also a roadway display of Minic models and another opportunity to try your skill, this time at flying a helicopter. There are cars and trams, a lifeboat and a (small) dinosaur, a display of clockwork boats (I used to have one of these!), and a rather more sophisticated model of the *Duchess of Fife* (a paddle steamer from the Clyde).

Perhaps the best display on this floor is that featuring Lego, from the early blocks right up to new pre-production kits – shown here in advance of full distribution. There are working Lego models too, ranging from space-age trains to a Saint Bernard dog complete with wagging tail. Before you leave this floor, do have a look at the 'loft layout'. Based upon the long defunct Welsh Highland narrow gauge line in North Wales, this evocative model shows what can be done in the limited space available to many model railway enthusiasts.

The Cumberland Toy and Model Museum is a fascinating place to visit and is ideal for all the family. Indeed, grandparents are a must for an explanation of some of the earlier exhibits. It is one of the few museums where you can hear the visitors talking to each other as they describe the toys they used to have as children. Perhaps the overriding impression it leaves is just how limited modern toys seem to be. Where are the toys that enable a young child's imagination to develop now? If ever there was an antidote to the TV culture it is to be found in this museum.

Wythop Mill
Embleton

Open Easter–October *Admission charge*

Hours 11.00–5.00, Sunday–Thursday

Address Wythop Mill, Embleton, Cockermouth, Cumbria CA13 9YP

Telephone (07687) 76394

Suitability for children 10 years and above.

Refreshments There is an excellent coffee shop on site.

Interest Industrial history, woodworking.

How to get there Wythop Mill is signposted off the A66 on the Keswick to Cockermouth section. There is no easy access by public transport.

Other attractions nearby Cumberland Toy and Model Museum (p. 44), Cumberland Pencil Museum (p. 68) and Keswick Museum and Art Gallery (p. 71).

Wythop Mill is one of the once numerous water-powered corn mills that were scattered around the County. Probably originating in the post-Norman period, the present mill was converted from a corn mill into a saw mill in the mid-nineteenth century. Its wooden waterwheel would have been replaced at that time by the hybrid one that exists today – 'hybrid' because it is made of a mixture of cast iron (for the rims and axle) and wood (for the linings and buckets).

As a saw mill, Wythop offers the visitor a very different experience from that to be gained at one of the preserved corn mills in the County (see p. 58). Wythop has something of the air of Stott Park Bobbin Mill (p. 121) about it, with displays concentrating on woodworking and blacksmithing.

Before entering the main building, take a look at the dam and sluice system which can be operated from inside the mill if necessary by means of ropes and pulleys. A walk around the back of the building reveals the overshot wheel, and some saw-mill machinery. There is an intriguing wheelwright display here too, with the manufacture of the various components of a cartwheel explained in some detail. It might be thought that the average cartwheel was constructed of just one type of wood – not so. The nave or central stock was made of elm; the spokes were of oak; and the felloes (rim) was made of ash, for no other wood could be trusted to take the punishment on an unsprung axle. The wheel held together thanks to the skill of the wheel-wright and the firmness of the joints he made – no glue was used.

On the ground floor of the mill itself we can see displays of old craft tools and a small room set out in the form of a miller's cottage. It is usefully labelled, and includes such items as orange slicers, a fish kettle and the ubiquitous posser (a sort of manual washing machine). You may also be intrigued by the rope-making device and the carding machine for horse hair.

Leaning in one corner of the downstairs room are some millstones which were discovered under the floor of the coffee shop during restoration – both the 'bedstone' and the 'runner' were found here. French burrstone was used for millstones. It is exceptionally hard, and essential where good white wheat flour is required. As an indicator of value, the stones cost £48 in 1838. At today's prices that's about £2,000!

Upstairs, past the tempting coffee shop, is a workshop space where various tools and machines illustrate the varied life the mill has had over the years. The waterwheel is still used to power belt-driven woodworking machines: devices such as a spindle moulder, a planer and thicknesser, a band saw and various lathes. When the wheel is under way you will be aware of the tremendous noise and vibration throughout the building. This is more marked than in some of the other local mills because the teeth on the cogs are made of iron rather than wood. Consequently the friction between them, even when well greased, is much greater. For anybody interested in old tools this upstairs room is a real treasure house. The walls are lined with weird and wonderful old-fashioned tools – an Archimedes drill, a socket bruzzer (?) and the obscure Forstner bit, to name but a few.

Wythop is very different to the other water-powered mills in Cumbria, specialising as it does in woodworking and crafts-manship. Its location is particularly attractive and the added bonus of a coffee shop makes it ideal for a family visit. If you're lucky you will see some of the machines working whilst you are there.

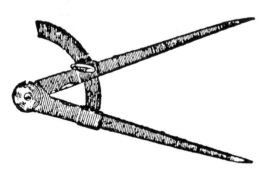

Helena Thompson Museum
Workington

Open All year *Admission free*

Hours April–October: 10.30–4.00, Monday–Saturday
November–March: 11.00–3.00, Monday–Saturday

Address Park End Road, Workington, Cumbria CA14 4DE

Telephone (0900) 62598

Suitability for children 10 years and above.

Refreshments In nearby town centre.

Interest Costume, local history.

How to get there Workington is accessible by rail and bus. The
railway station is about 20 minutes walk away, towards the harbour.
The bus station is on the corner of Murray Road and Oxford Street,
about 10 minutes walk away. You will find the museum on the A66
Cockermouth road. Parking is limited but there are pay and display
car parks in the town centre.

Other attractions nearby Maryport Maritime Museum (p. 41),
Senhouse Roman Army Museum (p. 38) and Whitehaven Museum
(p. 53).

Formerly known as Park End, the museum building was purchased by Helena Thompson in 1934. It was subsequently
bequeathed to the town, and eventually opened to the public
in 1949.

Entering via the main hall, you first come to the converted
drawing room which contains some of Miss Thompson's extensive costume collection, including a fine day dress in geranium
pink twilled silk, with voluminous sleeves and a delicate muslin
collar, dating from around 1830. There are also photographs of
various members of the Thompson family in dresses that are
too big to display – some crinoline dresses measure 15 feet
around the hem! Children's clothing is well displayed, with some

appealing babies' bonnets.

Other interesting items here include some Victorian women's accessories, such as jet jewellery and the skirt-lifters used to raise those yards of material clear of unsavoury pavements. Amongst the hats, look for the huge glazed cotton calash designed to cover more delicate headgear in bad weather.

Back across the hall is the former dining room, which contains some furniture and pictures from Helena Thompson's home. One of the miniatures depicts a Dr Joseph Read Marshall from Workington who became physician to the King of Naples.

The upstairs rooms are devoted to the history of Workington over the last 200 years, tracing the transformation of a small fishing and farming community into a nineteenth-century centre of coal-mining, iron- and steel-making and shipbuilding. The first room is dominated by a large model of Workington Hall (the real building is now sadly derelict). There is also a small display of farming-related items here, including shotguns, powder flasks and those curious knitting sheaths (the sort of thing you see in antique shops and can never quite identify).

In the main upstairs room shipbuilding is represented by a model of the locally built SS *Cliburn* (launched in 1916), and pottery by some items from the local works at Broughton and Clifton. The Clifton Dish is a particularly fine piece of slipware recently purchased by the museum. Coal-mining and the railways contribute some complex-looking mine-surveying equipment, whilst at the opposite end of the technological spectrum is a miner's lunch box, in which he would carry his 'snap' – a meal of bread and dripping or, on good days, jam.

Workington was, and still is, famous for its manufacture of high-quality rail track. This industry started in 1872 and relied on the mining of high-grade iron ore or haematite in the local area. The coal and iron mines have long since gone but the industry continues, importing the raw material and exporting its final product to all parts of the world.

Town life is depicted by displays on schooling. Look for the exercise book of John Wilson with its intricate mathematical diagrams, and for the large red banner of the Refuge Sunday

School. The temperance movement produced the vividly coloured ceremonial collars of the Independent Order of Rechabites, the oldest temperance fraternity in existence. The gallery also has a small display of civic regalia, including the town mace.

The Clifton Dish (courtesy of Allerdale District Council)

Local colour is added by photographs of local characters such as Freddie Cairns, the so-called 'Duke of Workington', seen selling his paper windmills. More exotic pursuits are represented by the 1913 visit of Gustav Hamel and his Bleriot aeroplane (which appears only marginally more robust than Freddie Cairns's windmills!).

Sporting achievement is not forgotten, a corner of the gallery being devoted to the innkeeper George Lowden and his Cumbrian Wrestling trophies.

This museum is a surprising discovery in the unremarkable surroundings of an old industrial town struggling to find a new direction. It also has a large temporary exhibition gallery, so check to see if there is something particularly interesting on.

Whitehaven Museum
Whitehaven

Open All year *Admission free*

Hours Monday–Saturday, 10.00–4.30

Address Civic Hall, Lowther Street, Whitehaven, Cumbria CA28 7SH

Telephone (0946) 693111 (Extension 307)

Suitability for children 10 years and above.

Refreshments There is a café in the Civic Hall building.

Interest Maritime history, coal-mining, social history.

How to get there Whitehaven is on the Cumbrian Coast line – the railway station is about 10 minutes walk away. Parking is available in the pay and display car parks near the museum.

Other attractions nearby Sellafield Visitor Centre (p. 56) and Helena Thompson Museum (p. 50).

Whitehaven may not seem an obvious tourist destination but the town has a remarkable history – it was at one time the third most important port in Britain – and its architectural heritage is of national importance. All this is admirably reflected in the local museum, despite its temporary accommodation in the Civic Hall.

You enter the museum gallery through a space devoted to temporary exhibitions, which could be on anything from Roman archaeology to paintings by local artists. As you walk into the main gallery you will notice a remarkable eighteenth-century enamelled glass goblet, the work of one William Beilby (or possibly his sister Mary, they were both outstanding artists). The goblet commemorates the launch of the Whitehaven-built slave trader *King George*.

Whitehaven's maritime history is enlivened by some colourful characters. John Paul Jones, for example, originally from

Scotland, arrived in Whitehaven to become an apprentice seaman in 1759. After a number of unhappy voyages he left for America, where he became known as 'The Founder of the American Navy'. During the American War of Independence he led a raid on Whitehaven Harbour, the last occasion on which an enemy power has forced a landing on the English mainland. There are various eighteenth-century exhibits relating to his exploits.

The Excise features heavily. There is an Excise officer's pistol of 1820, and a fascinating ledger of 1763 lists the officers then employed on Excise duty. The extensive social history related to shipping and trade is well represented too. There are certificates of ownership of Whitehaven vessels, seamen's discharge certificates, and a Master's certificate (belonging to a William Spedding) is carefully preserved along with its original metal case.

A model of SS *Hercules,* a nineteenth-century 1,155-ton cross-screw steamer, represents Whitehaven's shipbuilding industry, and various items of shipwreck memorabilia record brave rescues and triumphs over adversity. There are paintings too, and highly polished navigation instruments, as well as exotic evidence of worldwide trade: a samovar from Russia; a block of compressed tea and some shoes from China; gourds from the West Indies.

After the John Paul Jones incident Whitehaven suffered further naval interference during the First World War. A German submarine had the audacity to shell the ironworks at Lowca, causing quite a bit of damage and bringing forth a remarkable outpouring of anti-German prose and poetry by local residents.

Whitehaven's other great industries were coal- and iron-mining. Though the last pit at Haig Colliery closed in 1986, coal-mining is covered in detail at the museum, with miners' lamps, mine-surveying equipment, drills, detonators and fuses. Like seafaring, coal-mining had its tragedies, and Whitehaven perhaps had more than its fair share. There is a statuette presented by Czechoslovakian miners to their comrades at William Pit after the disaster there in 1947 when 104 men lost their lives. Medals and a letter from King George VI highlight the bravery of the rescue teams employed on these occasions.

Ancient history is also covered, and the most intriguing archaeological display concerns the St Bees burial. A medieval knight, apparently killed in the Crusades, was found well preserved in a lead coffin. The contents of the coffin were meticulously examined and the rather gruesome results are displayed here (although the unfortunate inmate has been returned to rest at St Bees).

All this historical meandering is brought sharply up to date by modern displays on the local chemical industry, and on British Nuclear Fuels. Finally there are some products of the local pottery industry, including the very fine Agate Ware candle lantern of 1865, made by John Kitchen.

Although these collections deserve far better accommodation, the rather uninviting surroundings cannot disguise the quality of this wonderful museum. The citizens of Whitehaven have a history to be proud of. The visitor to this museum can share in that history and leave enriched by the experience.

George III wine jug (courtesy of Copeland Borough Council)

Sellafield Visitor Centre
Seascale

Open All year *Admission free*

Hours April–October: 10.00–6.00, every day
November–March: 10.00–4.00, every day

Address British Nuclear Fuels plc, Visitor Centre, Sellafield,
Seascale, Cumbria CA20 1PG

Telephone (0946) 727027

Suitability for children All ages, though under-fives lacking a
grounding in nuclear physics may be bored!

Refreshments Good restaurant on site.

Interest Nuclear power.

How to get there Sellafield is off the A595 at Blackbeck, south of
Egremont. The recommended route from the M6 in summer is
from Junction 40 and through Cockermouth. There is good parking
on site. The railway station is about 2 miles away.

Other attractions nearby Ravenglass and Eskdale Railway
Museum (p. 61), Muncaster Mill (p. 63) and Eskdale Corn Mill
(p. 58). Also Muncaster Castle, the screes of Wastwater and some
excellent sand dunes at Drigg.

The Sellafield Visitor Centre is not, by any stretch of the imagination, a museum (or at least not yet). It is, however, a fantastic,
futuristic presentation of an industry that processes the waste
from nuclear power stations all over the world. The Centre is
run by British Nuclear Fuels who do not waste the opportunity
to present the whole story of nuclear power production from
the point of view of the electricity industry. Many visitors will
perhaps be surprised to learn that all nuclear energy is required
to do in power stations is to heat water to produce steam which
then drives the turbines, a rather mundane task for such a volatile
process.

Sellafield Visitor Centre uses all the latest techniques to get its message across. There are lots of interactive displays (with buttons to press), lifesize models of machinery and reactors, and plenty of videos to watch. The most spectacular item is probably the fission tunnel. As you walk through, clever use of mirrors creates a vision of a continuous atomic chain reaction, as well as rather disturbing multiple reflections of yourself stretching into infinity. There is also the curious experience of walking into the heart of a simulated Advanced Gas Cooled Reactor. Here you can watch as fuel rods are moved into the core of the reactor to increase the energy output.

Sellafield's visitor facilities can hardly be faulted – most museums would be grateful for just a small proportion of the resources available here. There are also free coach trips which take you on a tour into the heart of the works at Sellafield, but don't expect to learn any trade secrets about the industry.

The Sellafield plant is a dominant feature in West Cumbria, providing employment for many people in the area. If you have the opportunity then do visit it, and don't worry about radiation – you'll probably absorb a greater dose climbing in the Lakes, according to the brochures. Whatever your opinion on nuclear power and its waste disposal, this exhibition offers an opportunity to learn about the processes involved and to think about our ever-increasing energy consumption in this country.

Eskdale Corn Mill
Boot

Open Easter–September *Admission charge*

Hours 11.00–5.00, every day except Saturday

Address Boot, Holmrook, Eskdale, Cumbria CA19 1TG

Telephone (09403) 335

Suitability for children 10 years and above.

Refreshments Food is available at the village pubs or at the terminus of the Ravenglass and Eskdale Railway.

Interest Agricultural machinery and local history.

How to get there One of the best ways is to take the miniature railway from Ravenglass (next to the Cumbria Coast line) to its terminus at Dalegarth, then it's a ten-minute amble to the mill. Otherwise turn off the A595 west coast road at Gosforth and follow signs for Eskdale and Hardknott Pass. You can get there from Ambleside via the Pass, but be warned: this route is not for elderly cars or faint-hearted drivers!

Other attractions nearby Ravenglass and Eskdale Railway Museum (p. 61), Muncaster Mill (p. 63) and Sellafield Visitor Centre (p. 56).

Eskdale's milling history goes back a long way. It is first recorded in a local inventory of 1570, which states that one 'Robert Vicars holdeth a tenament, a barn and other buildings . . . and also the moiety of a water corn mill'. Owned by the Hartley family in the eighteenth century, the mill suffered a gradual decline in the mid-twentieth century when its last real function was to supply electricity, via a dynamo, to nearby Mill Cottage.

It was bought and restored by the County Council in 1972 and opened to the public in 1976. Although not yet fully working, a visit here can help you understand something of the technology that went into the apparently simple task of grinding corn. Today you first enter a room where the corn was dried prior to milling. The kiln lies below the floor. Fuelled by local peat, it is shaped like an inverted cone, and between the floor and the tiles (now metal but originally clay) is a metal baffle which helped distribute the heat. Grain would have been spread over the tiles to a depth of up to 5 inches, and dried for two to three hours depending on its dampness. Also in this room is a display of querns (grinding stones) and a pictorial history of the mill. Some milling and harvesting accessories are here too.

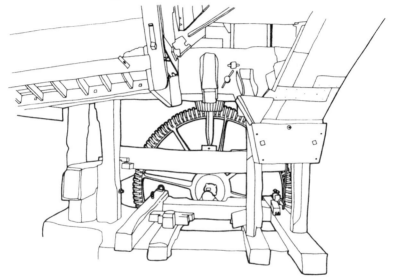

Mill machinery at Boot (courtesy of Cumbria County Council)

Moving on to the adjacent room we can see other types of milling machinery. Before the grain could be milled it had to pass through a wire dressing machine. This machine is essentially a cylinder of wire mesh driven by a belt from the waterwheel. Its blades dealt with any impurities and a fan blew away the dust. Once the grain was clean it was fed into a hopper above the stones, ready for grinding. The miller would then go downstairs, engage the millstones by lowering the applewood-toothed bevel wheel, open the sluice on the water channel and set the gate at the right height for the flow of water required. The various hoppers and the wheel itself could be controlled from inside the mill using ropes and pulleys. A wonderfully ingenious device also utilised the power of the main wheel to drive a hoist which raised sacks of grain up to the first floor; the trap doors in the floor even activated levers that automatically disengaged the drive mechanism!

Just off the main room is a small gallery where temporary exhibitions are often displayed, reflecting different aspects of life in this remote Lakeland valley. There are also displays of agricultural tools such as ploughs and hedge-trimmers as well as some explanations of how millstones were dressed. Like those at Wythop Mill (p. 47), the millstones here were made of French burrstone (graded blocks of a quartz-like stone cemented together and held by iron bands).

Outside the main mill building is the bakehouse, built by Edward Hartley in 1740. Like the corn-drying kiln, the oven was fuelled by peat from Boot Bank and the remains of the 'scales', used to store the dried peat, can still be seen on the hillside today.

A walk around the outside of the mill will reveal the two wheels used for milling here. The second wheel was added by Hartley in 1740 when the mill became underpowered for the additional activity it was taking on and there was too little space to enlarge the first wheel. Both wheels are of the overshot type which, though they are about 80 per cent efficient, do require a good head-race of water to drive them, and a good tail-race for the water to flow away.

Eskdale Mill and the surrounding hamlet and scenery evoke a picture of Lake District life that has all but disappeared beneath the weight of twentieth-century tourism. Try to imagine that you had reached Boot, not by car, but by horse or perhaps the old 3-foot gauge railway that ran up the valley to carry the iron ore away to the coast. Then, when you return to your home or hotel and bite into a slice of bread, consider the millers of old and their perfectly dressed millstones!

Ravenglass and Eskdale Railway Museum
Ravenglass

Open April–November (and some weekends out of season)
Admission charge

Hours 10.00–5.00, all week in season; weekends in February, March and November (or on request when trains are running)

Address Ravenglass and Eskdale Railway, Ravenglass, Cumbria CA18 1SW

Telephone (0229) 717171

Suitability for children All ages.

Refreshments Light snacks are available at the station café or you can get something more substantial at the Ratty Arms, the railway's own pub.

Interest Railway history and nostalgia.

How to get there Ravenglass is on the coast south of Sellafield, off the A595, and you can park at the station. The bus service is intermittent – the BR Cumbria Coast line is a lot better. Use it if you fancy a combined trip on the Ravenglass and Eskdale Railway – the two stations are just yards apart.

Other attractions nearby Sellafield Visitor Centre (p. 56), Muncaster Mill (p. 63) and Eskdale Corn Mill (p. 58). The Ravenglass area is particularly attractive and is well worth exploring.

The Ravenglass and Eskdale Railway, or 'La'al Ratty', opened in 1876 as a 3-foot gauge railway designed to carry iron ore from the mines up the Eskdale valley. For the next 30 years it was in desperate financial straits, its ever more decrepit rolling stock and engines wheezing up and down the valley.

In 1915 it was bought by a company interested in miniature railways, and the gauge was narrowed even further to 15 inches.

The 'Ratty' thus became a pleasure line, but one that still carried mineral traffic and indeed went on to build its own locomotives (a tradition still maintained today). After its chequered past the line now flourishes, transporting thousands of happy passengers up and down one of the most beautiful valleys in the Lake District.

This rich history is presented through objects, models and videos in a small but very entertaining museum at Ravenglass. The story of the iron-mining industry is retold, highlighting the way in which the 'red men' (so-called because of the colour of the haematite ore) mined the valuable mineral from the nearby fells. Little survives of the original 3-foot gauge railway but there are some wagon wheels and rail sections to be seen. Historic photographs supplement the information with wonderful pictures of slightly ramshackle trains.

The later 15-inch line is much better represented. The influence of W.J. Basset Lowke, the famous model engineer, is represented by the clockwork and live steam model trains, as well as the larger items used on the line itself. Old wagons and parts of carriages have been used to depict the early days of the pleasure railway; the style and quality is unmistakable, even down to the monogrammed china! Scenes from various parts of the railway are recreated in models, and an entertaining video describes the history of the line and takes us on a journey along the route.

As you leave the museum you will see *Synolga*, an early 15-inch gauge locomotive, a miniature version of one of the big main line expresses that once graced our railway system. In some respects the whole railway is a living museum. You will find nothing like it anywhere else in the north of England; it is an experience not to be missed.

Muncaster Mill
Ravenglass

Open April–October *Admission charge*

Hours April–May and September–October: 11.00–5.00, every day except Saturday
June–August: 10.00–6.00 (other times by appointment)

Address Muncaster Mill, Ravenglass, Cumbria CA18 1ST

Telephone (0229) 717232

Suitability for children All ages.

Refreshments There is a picnic area outside. Otherwise snacks are available in Ravenglass (about five minutes by car or you could take the steam train from the Mill station).

Interest Technology and local history.

How to get there The mill is located on the A595 south of Gosforth. The nearest British Rail station is at Ravenglass. You can then take the Ravenglass and Eskdale Railway to the mill.

Other attractions nearby Ravenglass and Eskdale Railway Museum (p. 61), Sellafield Visitor Centre (p. 56) and Eskdale Corn Mill (p. 58).

Muncaster Watermill is one of the few working water-powered mills in Cumbria that is still grinding corn. The present building dates from around 1700 but a mill has occupied the site since 1455 when it was recorded that Thomas Senhouse leased the mill for £3 a year from Sir John Pennington.

Today you enter the mill on the ground floor and immediately in front of you stands a mass of large cogged wheels which transfer the power from the waterwheel outside to the various pieces of machinery. A turn to the right will take you into the kiln area where the grain was dried before milling.

Before visiting the upper floors you should go outside to see the massive overshot waterwheel in action. The wheel is 12 foot

6 inches in diameter. It revolves at a slow but steady pace (about 6 rpm when I was there), and is left turning even when not milling. The water comes from the River Mite and is fed to the wheel along a $\frac{3}{4}$-mile-long manmade channel.

Retracing your steps from the wheel you finally enter the upper floor of the main building where the actual milling takes place. Here you can see the three pairs of stones and other related machinery. Today Muncaster Mill produces an excellent variety of stone-ground 100 per cent wholewheat flour which you can buy and take home to use in your own baking.

A visit to this mill takes you back to the pre-railway era when few communities were without at least one mill, either water- or wind-driven. Using the Ravenglass and Eskdale Railway to get there completes the nostalgic experience.

The mill wheel
(courtesy of the Eskdale
(Cumbria) Trust)

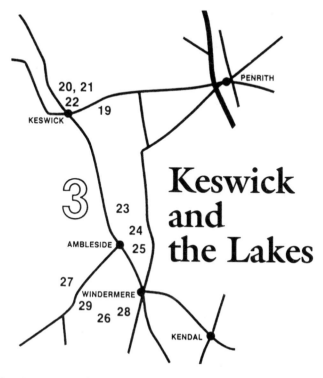

Keswick
and
the Lakes

19   Museum of Lakeland Mines and Quarries, Threlkeld *66*
20   Cumberland Pencil Museum, Keswick *68*
21   Keswick Museum and Art Gallery *71*
22   Cars of the Stars, Keswick *74*
23   Wordsworth Museum and Dove Cottage, Grasmere *77*
24   Rydal Mount, Ambleside *80*
25   Armitt Library and Museum, Ambleside *83*
26   Beatrix Potter Gallery, Hawkshead *85*
27   Ruskin Museum, Coniston *88*
28   Windermere Steamboat Museum *91*
29   Brantwood, Coniston *94*

Museum of Lakeland Mines and Quarries
Threlkeld

Address Threlkeld Quarry, Threlkeld, Near Keswick, Cumbria
Telephone (07687) 79747

This museum is due to open in 1992. For further information on opening contact one of the Cumbria Tourist Information Centres or phone the museum on the above number.

Located in a disused granite quarry (which has provided flag-stones for many a northern city), the museum will aim to tell the story of mining and quarrying in the Lakes from the earliest times. For over 5,000 years the rocks and minerals of the area have been exploited by man, starting with the 'axe factory' of the Neolithic farmers in Langdale. Nowadays the Cumbrian fells are still being exploited for granite and limestone. (You will see examples of recent quarries around Shap whilst travelling on the M6.)

The vernacular architecture of the County, the drystone walls and the natural features all owe something to the underlying geology of the fells. Without the veins of iron, copper, lead, graphite, zinc, barytes and cobalt, without the resources of fine slate and granite, towns such as Coniston and Keswick would still be small villages, though tourism would no doubt have had its effect.

The telling of this fascinating story has hitherto been left to museums with only small local geology collections. No single museum has previously attempted to cover the subject in depth, but Threlkeld is aiming to change all that. The proposed attractions are very exciting. There will be a gold-panning 'experience' where you will be able to search for real gold, and a Cumbrian iron ore mine 'experience'. Outside there will be a large display area devoted to some of the many items of equipment used in mines and quarries, from steam shovels to the various hand-held devices used to extract the precious ores and stones from the ground.

One prominent feature of the site will be a giant reconstructed waterwheel, over 30 feet in diameter, representing the main source of power in Cumbrian mines for many years. In the longer term there is a plan to rebuild the narrow-gauge mineral railway that originally ran from Threlkeld round to Bram Crag Quarry in St John's in the Vale.

If the unpredictable Lakeland weather gets too much for you there will be plenty to see indoors too. The intention is to interpret Threlkeld Quarry and its evolution from the eighteenth century, looking not just at the mining industry but also at the social history behind it and the effect it had upon the local scene. The Lakeland Mines and Quarries Trust are responsible for the development, and their archives will be housed in a newly built research library with a map and document collection.

Threlkeld Museum will be a major new contribution to the Cumbrian museum scene, offering something for all the family, whatever the weather. For the first time there will be a museum offering detailed information on the mines and quarries whose remains we can see all around us and whose products have shaped our modern environment.

Cumberland Pencil Museum
Keswick

Open All year *Admission charge*

Hours 9.30–4.00, every day

Address The Cumberland Pencil Company, Southey Works, Keswick, Cumbria CA12 5NG

Telephone (07687) 73626

Suitability for children All ages. The facility includes a play area for developing the artistic talents of younger children.

Refreshments There are plenty of cafés and pubs in the nearby town centre.

Interest Pencils and industrial archaeology.

How to get there The museum is located off Main Street, to the north-west of the town centre on the Cockermouth road. Turn off just before Greta Bridge. You can park outside the museum. The nearest railway station is at Penrith; there are good bus connections from there and Cockermouth.

Other attractions nearby Keswick Museum and Art Gallery (p. 71) and Cars of the Stars (p. 74). Or take a boat trip on Derwent Water or a good stiff walk up Skiddaw.

You wouldn't have thought that one of Cumbria's most successful museums could have been built around the humble pencil, but after a visit here you will look upon that simplest of drawing instruments in a new light! It is also the only museum in Cumbria where you enter the displays through a reconstructed underground mine tunnel.

Why do they make pencils in Keswick? The answer lies in the discovery of graphite (known locally as plumbago or wadd) in the nearby Borrowdale valley, which led to Keswick becoming the centre of the pencil industry in the last century. Graphite is one of the three naturally occurring forms of pure carbon and its properties make it ideal for making pencil leads (the Greek word *graphe* means 'writing' or 'inscription').

Having emerged from the tunnel, you are free to wander around the colourful exhibition, though it's worth sitting down in the video theatre for a few minutes to watch two interesting presentations. One is on the history of pencil-making in the area and the current production techniques; the other is an extract from the acclaimed Raymond Briggs cartoon 'The Snowman', which was drawn using Cumberland products.

The three main constituents of any pencil are the outer finish, the wooden casing and the core. The casing is Californian cedar, and there is a display explaining the production of the 'slats' which are made in California (over two million a day) and form the basis of the pencils made here. There is also a fascinating example of tree ring dating using a slice of cedar that is over 200 years old.

As for the use of local graphite in the cores, this came to an end when Conte began blending less superior graphite with clay to produce a more readily available substitute. Today, pencil cores can be made from a blend of waxes, gum, clay and pigment, the mixture depending on the product required. All the manufacturing processes are explained here, and you can see examples of some of the machinery. One of the machines puts the grooves in the slats and another shapes them into their final rounded form. There is also a painting machine – I was surprised to learn that pencils can have up to ten layers of paint on the outside, depending on the colour used! The last stage in the process is represented by the stamping machine that puts the lettering on the pencils, alas no longer in gold leaf.

There are displays of accessories for pencils, including attractive pencil boxes and those metal pencil tops that used to prevent you from spearing yourself as you reached into your top pocket. (Whatever happened to them?) A box of graphite used for polishing metal fire grates illustrates another use for this versatile material.

Colourful and imaginative displays show the vast range of pencils and crayons that have been produced over the years, going right back to the days of hand-made pencils produced by a substantial cottage industry in Keswick. A collection of photographs fills in the details of this early history, beginning with men such as John Ladyman who gave up the woollen trade 'to devote himself to pencil-making'. The origins of the Cumberland Pencil Company are, naturally, highlighted. The company is currently the major employer in Keswick and produces some of the world's finest pencils.

There are curiosities to be seen as well; look out for the green wartime pencils, for example. Wartime pencils were normally made without colour or lettering and these green pencils were produced in great secrecy. They are in fact partly hollow and originally contained a thin paper map and magnetic compass. The maps featured areas of Europe and were designed to help downed RAF crews to escape back to friendly territory. Such was the success of these pencils that the German forces never knew of their existence.

Having been thoroughly inspired by the videos and displays, you can satisfy your desire for drawing materials in the museum shop which is overflowing with all manner of pencils, crayons and paper. There is also a strategically placed gallery where you can let the children loose with the various products, and they can try some brass rubbing as well. Good marketing and a unique story have combined to produce one of the most interesting museums in the area, and the local industry it describes is still going strong in the factory nearby.

Keswick Museum and Art Gallery
Keswick

Open Easter–October *Admission charge*

Hours Tuesday–Sunday and Bank Holiday Mondays 10.00–4.00 (closed for lunch 12.00–1.00)

Address Station Road, Keswick, Cumbria CA12 4NF

Telephone (07687) 73263

Suitability for children 10 years and above. There's a play area for younger children in the park.

Refreshments There are many cafés and pubs in the nearby town centre.

Interest Local history, geology and natural history.

How to get there The museum is on Station Road in the centre of Fitz Park, on the east side of the town. There is street parking outside. The nearest railway station is at Penrith and there are good bus connections.

Other attractions nearby Cumberland Pencil Museum (p. 68) and Cars of the Stars (p. 74). Keswick Museum and Art Gallery has good recreational facilities in summer.

Keswick Museum was founded by the Fitz Park Trust in 1882 to 'provide rest and relaxation to the people of Keswick, and the visitors thereto'. Today it continues to do this very successfully through the well-kept park and gardens as well as the museum itself.

The Art Gallery, which was added in 1905, is used primarily for temporary exhibitions, usually of photographs and paintings, but it also has a section devoted to Lakeland literary figures. There are items related to Robert Southey's writing and life, including a flute of wood and silver, his leather gloves, and

71

various paintings of the poet and of the spectacular views from his home at Greta Hall, Keswick. Sir Hugh Walpole, who lived at Brackenburn near Derwent Water, is perhaps best remembered for the series of novels called 'The Herries Chronicles', based largely in Cumberland. There is a case of original manuscripts for these novels neatly bound in fine leather. In addition, there are a number of smaller displays in the Art Gallery: Victorian jewellery; albums of photographs by Sir Oswald Simkin; and a handwritten journal by a young woman from Hull who visited the Lakes in 1859. Two fine oil paintings, *Skaters on Derwent Water* and *Keswick Street*, both by Joseph Brown Junior and dated around 1870, are exhibited here too.

The next room, the Natural History Gallery, is dominated by the large model of the Lake District made by Joseph Flintoft in the early nineteenth century. It took him 17 years to build. The rest of this gallery is lined with displays of wildlife that can, or could formerly, be found in the area. Sadly, most of these specimens have seen better days and can be passed quickly by (although children seem to like them). More interesting are the cabinets containing trays of butterflies and moths that can be pulled out, *gently*, to reveal their vibrant colours.

The main gallery contains many items from the museum's extensive geological collection, including rocks, and fossils, and beautiful minerals from the local mines, particularly those of the Carrock Fell and Caldbeck area. There are archaeological exhibits too, although you may find it difficult to discover where they come from. Prehistoric axes, Roman pottery and quernstones (for grinding corn) all vie for attention.

A unique family record is preserved in the form of a window shutter carved by one John Watson who recorded his family's marriages on it in 1663. Elsewhere Jonathan Otley, early guidebook author, botanist, geologist and meteorologist, is represented by some of his surveying instruments. There are also the belongings of the unfortunate Earl of Derwent Water, beheaded in 1716.

The star of the collection has to be the famous mummified cat. Over 500 years old, it was found trapped in the roof space of Clifton Church, where it had died of starvation. This rather gruesome exhibit is discreetly hidden inside an old wooden chest. There are other curiosities to be found too: a wooden porridge bowl; small cannons (probably used in the regattas on Derwent Water); Napoleon's cup and saucer; and finally some lion's teeth! The local graphite-mining and pencil-making industry is represented by a small but effective display that includes the original 'Big Pencil' of 1858.

There is an unusual opportunity for visitor participation with the musical stones. Brought together between 1840 and 1900 by the Richardson family, they form a 'geological xylophone' which you can play for yourself. Finally there is a collection of dolls from all over the world donated to the museum in 1948.

Keswick Museum and Art Gallery exists in a world of its own, having remained virtually unchanged for decades. It is not a place for the visitor who expects modern displays or facilities, but it *is* a classic example of a truly local museum, and a place in which to let your imagination do the work.

Cars of the Stars
Keswick

Open Easter–December *Admission charge*

Hours 10.00–5.00, every day

Address Standish Street, Town Centre, Keswick, Cumbria CA12 5LS

Telephone (07687) 73757

Suitability for children All ages.

Refreshments Available at the museum.

Interest Motor vehicle history, TV and film nostalgia.

How to get there The museum is located down a side street in the south-east end of town. There are pay and display car parks in Victoria Street and Heads Road. The nearest railway station is at Penrith and there are good bus connections.

Other attractions nearby Keswick Museum and Art Gallery (p. 71) and the Cumberland Pencil Museum (p. 68).

This recent addition to the Cumbrian museum scene is more an exhibition than a museum, but let's not be too pedantic. Where else can you see James Bond's Lotus alongside Del Boy's Robin Reliant?

The main aim is to present the changing role of vehicles in film and TV, and thus the display starts, logically enough, with the ubiquitous Model-T Ford of 1923 and a very angular-looking curved-dash Oldsmobile of 1902. Both were familiar sights in the early silent films, and Laurel and Hardy were just two of the stars whose pictures often featured scenes using the Model-T (often with terminal results for the car!).

Also of considerable age is the actual Morris 8 Tourer used in the popular BBC TV series *All Creatures Great and Small*. This example dates back to 1933 and seems remarkably small even compared with the smaller hatchbacks of today. Main-

74

taining the theme of compactness is the curious Fiat Gamine of 1972, affectionately known as 'the Noddy Car'. The example displayed here has been painted in the same colours as Noddy's own car in the much-loved children's picture books.

Two of the types of vehicles used in the cult TV series *The Prisoner* are featured. You will see the Lotus Super 7 driven by 'No. 6' (Patrick McGoohan) in the London scenes; a car described as 'fast, noisy, draughty and uncomfortable – but enormous fun to drive'. The Mini Moke of 1965 was used as Village transport in the series, filmed on location at Portmeirion in North Wales. Only 1,500 Mini Mokes were ever registered in Britain and production was transferred to Australia in 1968. More recent motorised 'TV stars' are the actual 1947 Triumph Roadster driven by Jim Bergerac in the series of that name set in Jersey, and the Mark II Jaguar used in the Liverpool series *Bread*.

A vehicle with a very different history is the American-built 1927 Graham Paige, originally owned by a Mr Wallace. It was shipped to this country in the 1930s when its owner attempted to set up a gangster-style protection racket. The Metropolitan Police soon put a stop to that, however, and the owner returned to the US, leaving the car in a garage in Surrey for many years. It underwent a major restoration in 1965.

Another car with an exciting history is the Ford Escort RS 1600 built in 1972. It was the winner of the 1972 East African Safari Rally and was driven by Hannu Mikkala and Gunnar Palm. Despite that, and later rally experiences, the car shows remarkably little damage.

Novelties from the extremes of vehicle design are well represented: there's Del Boy's Robin Reliant from the BBC TV series *Only Fools and Horses*; the curious Messerschmitt KR175 of 1961 (a cult vehicle in its time); and, looking very forlorn, Clive Sinclair's brave little C5.

The museum also includes vehicles from the fantasy world of espionage: the original Volvo P1800 driven by Roger Moore, alias Simon Templar, in *The Saint*; the Lotus Espirit Turbo (prototype) used in the Bond movie *For Your Eyes Only*; and for the older Bond fans amongst us, an Austin Martin DB5 similar to that used by Connery in the earlier films. If any of us care to admit remembering as far back as the TV series *The Avengers*, the original Lotus driven by Emma Peel is here too.

The cars in this museum are well displayed, with some care being given to recreating the correct atmosphere for each vehicle. Though the museum is unashamedly directed at the tourist market, it provides facilities and displays that can be enjoyed by all the family, and new exhibits are being added all the time.

Chitty Chitty Bang Bang, a prize acquisition

Wordsworth Museum and Dove Cottage
Grasmere

Open February–December *Admission charge*

Hours 9.30–5.00, every day

Address Town End, Grasmere, Ambleside, Cumbria LA22 9SG

Telephone (09665) 544

Suitability for children 10 years and above.

Refreshments There's a good restaurant by the main museum car park.

Interest Literary history and fine art.

How to get there The museum is just off the A591, south of the village. There is parking on site. The nearest railway station is at Windermere, and there are buses from Ambleside and Keswick.

Other attractions nearby The Armitt Library in Ambleside (p. 83) and the Windermere Steamboat Museum (p. 91). Grasmere village and lake are very picturesque and there is some excellent walking in the area.

Dove Cottage was William Wordsworth's home from 1799 to 1808, and it was here that some of his most famous works were completed. The cottage itself dates back to the early seventeenth century. Built of local stone with limewashed walls and a slate roof, it has been furnished in a style suited to Wordsworth's time, and includes some interpretative displays. The popularity of the place is such that entrance has to be regulated.

The excellent museum dedicated to Wordsworth and the English Romantics is cleverly incorporated into an old building behind the present museum shop (where you will need to buy your tickets). You enter by way of a small orientation lobby where a receptionist will provide information on the exhibits.

To the right is an Introductory Room which features changing displays related to the central theme. You will find the variety of objects and pictures stunning. When I paid my visit this room had some intriguing items used by eighteenth-century artists attempting to capture Lakeland landscape. To use the Claude Glass, for example, you had to stand facing the opposite direction! The glass would then reflect and frame the view over your shoulder.

William and Dorothy Wordsworth

Moving on from the curiosities on the ground floor, there are several pictures lining the stairwell. Farington's pencil and wash view of Grasmere is particularly fine. At the top of the stairs is an interesting item called Spooner's Transformation No. 7. By pressing a switch you can back-light an image of two cockerels fighting and impose the heads of Napoleon and Wellington on to the birds – an early piece of political satire.

Opposite you will see a reconstruction of a statesman farmer's kitchen or 'houseplace' of around 1700. Some of the furniture and utensils that would have been used in Dove Cottage are displayed here. The ornate bread cupboard was once common, and can still be found in some Lakeland farms. Note also the rush lights and the wool-weaving accessories.

In the main gallery are the real treasures associated with Wordsworth. A set of headphones allows you to listen to extracts of poetry, adding greatly to the experience. There are objects used and collected by Wordsworth. His ice skates, for example, bring to mind the lines from his autobiographical poem 'The Prelude': 'All shod with steel/We hissed along the polished ice, in games/Confederate, imitative of the chase . . .'. Other items include Wordsworth's scarf, cloak and waistcoat; some pistols belonging to his son John; and some boxes of hair taken as a memento of his daughter Dora after her death in 1847.

It is the manuscripts, books and paintings, however, that really bring you close to the man. Here you can see the scribbled lines of poetry with the corrections and notes all clearly legible. Here also is Dorothy's wonderfully meticulous journal which gives us so much insight into life at the cottage, and which helped inspire some of her brother's famous poems.

It was on Wordsworth's return from Germany in 1799 that he first saw Dove Cottage with his close friend Samuel Taylor Coleridge, and by December of that year he and Dorothy had taken up residence. Dove Cottage was to be visited by many of their friends over the years, including Thomas De Quincey, and Coleridge (described by Wordsworth as 'the most wonderful man I have ever known'). The increasing number of these friends persuaded Wordsworth, now married with a growing family, to move first to Allan Bank in Grasmere; then to the Vicarage; and finally to Rydal Mount where he lived out the rest of his life.

Dove Cottage and the Wordsworth Museum are places where we can gain a real sense of another age, and their task is very specific – to interpret the work of William Wordsworth and the Romantic Movement. To many, this legacy is as important a part of our heritage as the Tower of London or Stonehenge.

Rydal Mount
Ambleside

Open All year *Admission charge*

Hours March–October: 9.30–5.00, every day
November–February: 10.00–4.00, every day except Tuesday

Address Rydal, Ambleside, Cumbria LA22 9LU

Telephone (05394) 33002

Suitability for children 10 years and above.

Refreshments There's a pub at the bottom of the hill, below the house. Otherwise it's best to go into Ambleside.

Interest Literary history.

How to get there Rydal Mount is on the A491, north of Ambleside, on the way to Grasmere. There is parking on site. Buses from Ambleside to Keswick pass by the bottom of the hill, about 200 yards away.

Other attractions nearby Wordsworth Museum and Dove Cottage (p. 77), Armitt Library (p. 83) and Rydal Water.

William and Mary Wordsworth moved into Rydal Mount on May Day 1813. They were accompanied by Dorothy (William's sister) and Sara Hutchinson (his sister-in-law).

Early in 1813 William had been appointed Distributor of Stamps in the County of Westmorland. This released him from financial worries and enabled him to live at Rydal in reasonable comfort. He was to live there for 37 years, until his death in 1850.

Today the house is open to the public as a monument to one of the country's best-known poets. Despite its proximity to Dove Cottage (p. 77) the atmosphere is very different. Here is a family home still occupied by Wordsworth's descendants, so don't be too put off by the rather modern touches in some of the rooms!

As you enter the dining room, the most noticeable feature is the spice cupboard set in one wall. This was created by Edward Knott whose family owned Rydal from 1700 to 1780, and whose son Michael extended the house in 1750. There are various engravings of Wordsworth and his daughter Dora on the walls. There is also a manuscript of the sonnet 'On a portrait of the Duke of Wellington upon the field at Waterloo, by Haydon'. A print of the original painting hangs nearby (it was presented to Wordsworth by the artist).

Going into the library, you will see a portrait of Dorothy hanging above the fireplace. This was painted by S. Crosthwaite in 1833 when Wordsworth's sister was 63. At the time Dorothy had more or less recovered from a serious bout of mental illness but there were frequent relapses and she had a complete breakdown three years later.

You can walk directly through from the library into the drawing room (they were knocked into one in 1968). It is a large light room with a superb view towards Windermere. In one corner of the room stands a small statue, 'The Curious Child', which was owned by Wordsworth and is mentioned in Book IV of 'The Excursion'. The portrait of the poet by Henry Inman was commissioned when Wordsworth became Poet Laureate. This room also contains some personal Wordsworth memorabilia: a letter case inscribed W.W.; an inkstand; and a breakfast condiments set. An interesting item is the cigar case decorated with various tea company crests.

Upstairs on the first landing is William and Mary's bedroom, which contains portraits of Queen Victoria and the Prince of Wales, and a photograph of the poet's grandson Gordon Wordsworth. From the window can be seen a corner of Dora's Field and Rydal Church. Wordsworth bought the field at a time when he thought he might be turned out of Rydal Mount and might need to build a house on it. When this proved unnecessary he gave the field to Dora and every spring it blooms with daffodils planted in her memory when she died in 1847. Today it belongs to the National Trust.

The next bedroom is Dora's. On the wall hangs a small

watercolour believed to have been painted by her, and a photograph of her field. Next door is Dorothy's bedroom.

The study, which was probably added to the house around 1838, is up another flight of stairs. The ceiling is a copy of one that Wordsworth admired in Italy on his second tour of the continent and the room contains some interesting items relating to Wordsworth and his family. Wordsworth's younger brother John was Captain of an East Indiaman, the *Earl of Abergavenny*. In 1804 the ship was attacked by the French. The English defeated their attackers, and in appreciation of the action Lloyds of London presented the Captain of each East Indiaman with a sword. John's sword is on display here. He died a year later when his ship ran aground off Portland Bill during a gale.

John Wordsworth's sword

In a central display case are lots of books that have some association with Wordsworth. One interesting example is a volume from Southey's 'Cottonian Library'. (All these books were covered with fabric from various women's dresses and petticoats!) Lastly, you will notice that one wall of the room is completely filled with a huge genealogical table.

Rydal Mount is very different from the other Wordsworth exhibitions to be found in the Lakes. Its charm lies in its situation – one of the best in Lakeland – and the fact that it still feels like a family home. There are some attractive gardens here too, designed by Wordsworth and little changed since his day. Before leaving, do call in on the small shop which is located in Dora's schoolroom, the former saddle-room above the stable.

Armitt Library and Museum
Ambleside

Open All year *Admission free*

Hours By appointment

Address The Armitt Library, Ambleside, Cumbria LA22 0BZ

Telephone (05394) 33949

Suitability for children 10 years and above.

Refreshments There is plenty of choice in Ambleside.

Interest Topography, geology, archaeology, rare books and literary history.

How to get there The Armitt Library is located above the public library in Ambleside. The nearest railway station is at Windermere and there are buses from Windermere and Keswick.

Other attractions nearby The tiny Bridge House (owned by the National Trust), and ferry trips on Lake Windermere. The town is also an excellent base for walks in the surrounding fells. If you're keen on gardening then the extensive Hayes Garden World in Lake Road will be worth a visit.

The Armitt Library contains much that represents the best of literary Lakeland. At first sight the room that houses the collection seems overcrowded, with books, artefacts and paintings jostling for attention. Do not be put off, however, for this is a treasure house of rare and beautiful things.

The library owes its existence to Mary Armitt who bequeathed her own collection of books to the people of Ambleside in 1912. The library and museum quickly grew, absorbing other local collections from the Ambleside Book Society and the Ambleside Ruskin Society (founded in 1882).

Many famous literary figures became members of the library or are represented by their descendants and relatives. The writer Harriet Martineau's niece Harriet Higginson donated copies of her aunt's books. Arthur Ransome, of *Swallows and Amazons* fame, and the historian philosopher R.G. Collingwood were amongst its distinguished users. The influence of John Ruskin is reflected in his collection of over 400 mineral specimens. There are also valuable Ruskin letters which were acquired from the successor to Ruskin's doctor. They reveal yet another writer and philosopher heavily dependent on 'tonic', the rather discreet term for opium.

Beatrix Potter's children's illustrations are of course well known but few of us are perhaps aware of her superb water-colours of botanical specimens, archaeological objects and fossils. The Armitt Library owns the largest collection of such work by 'BP'. She became a library member after her marriage to William Heelis, a trustee, and went on to donate many fine books which reflect her tastes and indicate some of the influences on her own work.

Visitors to this library should not expect to find 'instant history'; it is a place for patient exploration to discover new facts about the literary figures associated with the area and to view collections of archaeological and geological material from the Ambleside district.

Harriet Martineau, 1833

Beatrix Potter Gallery
Hawkshead

Open April–November *Admission charge*

Hours 10.30–4.00, Monday–Friday

Address Main Street, Hawkshead, Cumbria LA22 0NS

Telephone (09666) 355

Suitability for children All ages.

Refreshments There's a good choice available in adjacent streets.

Interest Children's literature, fine art, farming and conservation.

How to get there You will find the gallery in the main square in Hawkshead. Parking is in a large pay and display car park about 5 minutes walk away, near the National Park Information Centre. The nearest railway station is Windermere, and there is a bus connection from there.

Other attractions nearby Hawkshead Courthouse (owned by the National Trust), Windermere Steamboat Museum (p. 91) and the Armitt Library (p. 83).

The Beatrix Potter Gallery is housed in the former office of her husband, the solicitor William Heelis, and the interior has remained largely unchanged since his day. The Heelis office was well situated, in Main Street near the police station, next to an inn and opposite the bank! Its previous owners included a joiner, a linen draper, a grocer, and a hooper who lived in the house next door, amusingly called 'Bend or Bump'. The accommodation was compact and convenient for a firm of solicitors, the partners cloistered upstairs and the clerks down below. The atmosphere appears to have been busy and cheerful, the clerks keeping up their spirits by recording events such as marriage and war service on the back of a cupboard door downstairs. The building passed into the hands of the National Trust in 1946, but continued to be rented by the firm of Gatey and Heelis until 1986.

Today it forms a wonderfully intimate gallery devoted to the artistic talents of Beatrix Potter, concentrating mainly on her children's storybook illustrations. Having bought tickets from a separate office, you enter on the ground floor. The main display here is a reconstruction of William Heelis's office, including some of the original furnishings and bookcases full of rather tedious-looking legal tomes.

Going up the narrow staircase to the next floor, you will find some of the delightful watercolours painted by Beatrix Potter over the years to illustrate her children's stories. The exhibition changes annually so that each delicate painting is not exposed to too much light, and also to allow as many as possible of the 700 or so works to be displayed in sequence. One unusual exhibit is an anti-free trade poster dating from the First World War, painted by 'BP'. There are also two Delmar Bonner portraits of Beatrix here: one as a young woman; the other showing her in later life.

The rooms upstairs are well laid out, allowing plenty of space to view the paintings. The lighting is subtle and very sophisticated, minimising the heat and light damage to the works. Here are all the old favourites: Jemima Puddle Duck, Tom Kitten, Samuel Whiskers, Peter Rabbit, of course, and many others. It was after moving to the Lakes and buying Hill Top Farm at Sawrey that Beatrix began to use local views and holiday sketches, originally done at Lingholm near Keswick, in her books. Copies of many of the famous children's books (published by Frederick Warne) are thoughtfully laid out on tables in the gallery rooms so that you can read the stories in full.

After her marriage to William Heelis, Beatrix Potter became less interested in writing and more involved in farming. Indeed her last two books, *Fairy Caravan* and *Little Pig Robinson*, can largely be seen as patchworks of old ideas. Her farming activity is well represented downstairs by some photographs of the properties she bought and subsequently bequeathed to the National Trust. Whenever she could she added to her land holdings, preventing estates from being broken up and protecting farmland from development. In 1923 she greatly increased her standing in the local farming community by buying the magnificent Troutbeck Park Farm, together with its large flock of Herdwick sheep and almost 2,000 acres of fell grazing.

The Beatrix Potter Gallery. Hawkshead

Before long she was a well-known sheep breeder and the first woman president of the Herdwick Sheep Breeders Association. It was through Canon Rawnsley, who helped to found the National Trust in the late nineteenth century, that Beatrix Potter came to see her own land purchases as a way of preserving her property in perpetuity. She often sold her drawings to fund land purchases for the Trust, and eventually bequeathed it 14 farms and over 4,000 acres of land.

The Beatrix Potter Gallery is a delightful place. The pictures it contains are fondly remembered elements of many a visitor's childhood, and not surprisingly they remain as popular today as they were over 50 years ago. Do not forget the other side of Beatrix Potter's life however: the generosity that protected so much of the stunning scenery we now enjoy. Without her foresight, how much of modern Lakeland would have remained free of destructive development?

Ruskin Museum
Coniston

Open Easter–October *Admission charge*

Hours 9.30–5.30, every day

Address The Institute, Yewdale Road, Coniston, Cumbria

Telephone (05394) 41541

Suitability for children 10 years and above.

Refreshments Available in nearby pubs and cafés.

Interest Literature, fine art and local history.

How to get there The museum is located on the road out of Coniston toward Ambleside, opposite the fire station. The nearest railway station is at Ulverston, with buses from there and Ambleside.

Other attractions nearby Brantwood (p. 94), Coniston Copper Mines and the *Gondola* Steam Yacht. If you're feeling fit try climbing the Old Man!

The Ruskin Museum in Coniston is one of the gems of the Lake District and, dating back to 1884, one of the oldest museums in Cumbria. Despite its name the museum actually covers much more than Ruskin. Its displays and collections illustrate many aspects of the history of Coniston and the surrounding area.

You will read more about John Ruskin under the entry for Brantwood (p. 94), his former home, but suffice to say here that Ruskin was a great influence on this museum's early development. He presented a collection of 124 mineral specimens to the museum in its early days, and other friends and colleagues soon followed his example. W.G. Collingwood, Ruskin's secretary and biographer and a noted antiquarian, became an active member of the Institute committee, and some of Collingwood's paintings and archaeological discoveries can be seen amongst the displays.

Today the museum is housed in a slightly forbidding room at the rear of the Institute building. On entering you are immediately aware of the paintings and drawings that line the walls, and the display cases full of curios, seemingly placed at random around the room. All the pictures, some of which are engravings or prints, are associated with Ruskin and his 'circle' in some way.

The work of Ruskin is worth looking at in detail. See if you can find *Sunset at Jerusalem on the Longest Day*, painted as if from a viewpoint in space, with the sun's shadow falling across Jerusalem. There are fine watercolours, such as *Study of Tintoretto's Miracle of Saint Mark*, and superb pencil sketches – *Godstow – Oxford 1838* is just one example.

An impression of the extraordinary character of this artist philosopher can be gained from the photographs of him, as well as the copies of some of his correspondence. He was a well-travelled man and many of the pictures in the collection are views of Italy; Venice in particular. He also collected abroad, and a number of artefacts, such as a small and delicate column which he rescued from restoration debris at the Church of St Mary of the Thorn in Pisa, reflect this. The many beautiful and varied geological specimens displayed illustrate Ruskin's interest in geology, particularly his published work on 'banded' and 'brecciated' rock.

One of Ruskin's legacies in this part of Cumbria was a particular linenwork style called Ruskin Linen (known locally as Greek lace). With the help of a Miss Twelves and the support of the Guild of St George it developed as a recognised art, and the technique is still taught today. At Ruskin's funeral, in January 1900, his pall was made from Ruskin Linen by Miss Twelves, and it can now be seen at the Museum.

But what of the other Coniston artefacts? W.G. Collingwood's activities and interests are represented by several archaeological finds: two Bronze Age burial urns from the stone circle at Banniside; material from various Roman sites including Hardknott Fort above Eskdale (well worth a visit in itself); and pottery from Peel Island on Coniston Water. Curiously, the archaeological display case is lined with genuine William Morris wallpaper taken from Beatrix Potter's bedroom at Hill Top Farm.

The theme of water transport links the two very different displays. The first concerns *Gondola*, a fine example of Victorian transport, and a perfect combination of Venetian gondola and English steam yacht. Her fine lines graced Coniston Water from 1859 to 1939 after which she fell into disrepair and lay idle for many years. She was then restored by Vickers Shipbuilders in Barrow and returned to service in 1980 by the National Trust. She provides *the* way to travel on Coniston and a voyage on her is not to be missed. A large model of *Gondola* can be seen in the museum.

Donald Campbell's attempt at the water speed record ended in tragedy on 4 January 1967. He had reached a speed of 310 mph when *Bluebird* somersaulted and disintegrated. Campbell's body was never found. There is a pictorial history of the various attempts made at the record on Coniston Water including the dramatic pictures from that final run.

For me the most entertaining exhibits are the musical stones given to Ruskin (see also Keswick Museum and Art Gallery (p. 71)) and the strange seal cut from the fingertip of a specimen of chalcedony – the motto reads 'Today, Today, Today'.

The Ruskin Museum is small even by Cumbrian standards, but it represents a very valuable impulse which strove to provide education for the masses, owing its existence to the Mechanics' Institutes movement of the mid-nineteenth century. When you visit it try to leave behind the usual expectations of the tourist. This museum was created for the education of the copper miners of the area, it is a truly local museum, and should be treated with the respect it deserves.

 Ruskin's seal

Steamboat Museum
Windermere

Open Easter–October *Admission charge*

Hours 10.00–5.00, every day

Address Rayrigg Road, Bowness on Windermere, Cumbria LA23 1BN

Telephone (09662) 5565

Suitability for children All ages.

Refreshments There is a kiosk at the museum.

Interest Water transport and local history.

How to get there The museum is just off the A592, north of the Windermere car ferry at Ferry Nab. The nearest railway station is at Windermere, but you'll need to get a bus to the museum – Bowness buses will do.

Other attractions nearby Lakeside and Haverthwaite Railway (p. 123) and the Beatrix Potter Gallery (p. 85).

This wonderful museum is divided into a large exhibition gallery and a 'wet dock' built out over Lake Windermere. The exhibition gallery displays a wide variety of sailing and motor-driven craft, mostly associated with the lake in some way.

The earliest exhibit is part of a sailing yacht believed to have been built at Whitehaven in 1780 for the Curwen family of Belle Isle. Armed only with an old photograph, the museum's founder George Pattinson set out one morning to find the yacht in Southport. By evening he had found it, lying upside down in a field and being used as a hen house! The craft was promptly exchanged for some sheets of corrugated iron for the homeless hens.

Other early craft displayed in this gallery include some canoes, such as the *Rob Roy* of 1870. The name comes from John 'Rob Roy' Macgregor who travelled extensively in Africa and the

Middle East in just this type of craft. Another small vessel is the flat-bottomed boat that once belonged to Beatrix Potter. It was recovered from Moss Eccles Tarn and presented to the museum in 1976.

There are some more advanced water craft to be seen here too. *Miss Windermere IV*, for example, holds the 111.73 mph water speed record for a hydroplane, achieved in 1971. This is not surprising, perhaps, since she is powered by a Jaguar E-Type engine. Another hydroplane racer called *Cookie* featured at the Boat Show in 1963; she has a Volvo 1800cc engine.

The rest of the hall is filled with displays covering aspects of life on Windermere, and some of the personalities associated with the Lake. Colonel G.J.M. Ridehalgh, for example, was the owner of the 107-foot *Britannia*, the largest steam yacht ever built for the lake. She originally cost around £12,000 and some of the fine china used on board is displayed here.

Jack Kitchen was another local personality. Something of an inventor, he was responsible for creating, amongst other things, the reversing rudder, the Lune Valley boiler (which sounds rather like a barn dance!), and a gas-powered gramophone.

Before leaving the hall cast your eyes upwards to the glider hanging from the roof. Windermere had a pioneering role in developing aircraft that landed and took off from water. In 1911 the first aircraft of this type took off from the lake and in 1943 the first glider.

Moving away from the gallery and through the shop area, you enter a real 'Aladdin's Cave', a dock full of gleaming exhibits. The visual pleasure of the polished brass and mahogany are complemented by the sound of gently lapping water.

It seems unfair to highlight any of these beautiful craft but I shall mention just a few. S.L. *Kittiwake* and S.L. *Water Viper* are two examples of the stylish steam launches used on the lake. S.L. *Kittiwake* has recently been restored and converted back to steam using the original engine which was discovered in North Wales. S.L. *Otto*, launched in 1896, is, if anything, even finer: a powerful boat with a sleek steel hull that allowed a speed of 18 mph.

There are some more examples of motor boats here too, such as the 1930s M.V. *Raea*, with her novel streamlined cabin. M.V. *Canfly* is a unique boat, powered by a Rolls Royce 4 litre Hawk engine originally made for an airship in 1917. She was capable of 30 mph and the only means of stopping her was to kill the engine and drift to a halt.

Moored outside the ship hall is T.S.S.Y. *Esperance*, the oldest vessel on Lloyd's Yacht Register. She was built in 1869 for the great Furness industrialist H.W. Schneider, and he used her to commute daily from Bowness to Barrow. Since she was expected to sail in all weathers her bow was heavily raked to break light ice. *Esperance* is best known for her role as Captain Flint's houseboat in Arthur Ransome's book *Swallows and Amazons*, and she was used as such in the recent BBC film.

In the Windermere Steamboat Museum the social history of England's largest lake is inextricably linked with the stories behind the various boats displayed. For the children, there's a model boat pond (a lively programme of summer events includes model boat rallies). The museum also runs regular trips from the pier on their steam launches. This is an excellent way of experiencing the elegance and grace of these craft, and you'll be surprised at the quietness of the ride!

The steam launch *Dolly*, 1850

93

Brantwood
Coniston

Open All year *Admission charge*

Hours Mid-March–mid-November 11.00–5.30, every day
Mid-November–mid-March 11.00–4.00, Wednesday–Sunday

Address Brantwood, Coniston, Cumbria LA21 8AD

Telephone (05394) 41396

Suitability for children 10 years and above.

Refreshments There is an excellent cafe – The Jumping Jenny – in the grounds.

Interest Literature, fine art and philosophy.

How to get there Brantwood is on the East Lakeside Road from Ulverston. Buses run to Coniston from Ulverston and Ambleside. The best, and most stylish, way to get to the house is by the steam yacht *Gondola* from Coniston pier (Easter–November).

Other attractions nearby The Ruskin Museum (p. 88), the steam yacht *Gondola* and Grizedale Forest sculpture trail.

When Ruskin came to live at Brantwood he was 53 and at the height of his fame. Though chiefly remembered for his work on economics and social welfare, he was also a poet and an accomplished artist, producing superb watercolours and pencil sketches. His anger at the condition of the working class in Victorian England led him to write *Unto This Last*, a work of great force and passion. This book in particular caused Ruskin to be dubbed a revolutionary by his opponents.

Today Brantwood house and gardens have been opened to the public by the Bembridge Trust. Apart from the tremendous views and the impressive collection of Ruskin memorabilia there is a gallery devoted to the late A. Wainwright, the producer of those ubiquitous Lakeland Guides, and a tea room called The Jumping Jenny (named after Ruskin's rowing boat). However it is the house itself that draws you on, a seemingly random collection of rooms, vastly different from the humble cottage built here in 1797.

Having passed through the shop, you will find a video room to your right where you can see a potted history of the man and his times. Ahead lies the first of a number of rooms lined with Ruskin's artistic works. Everywhere you are reminded of his phrase 'There is no wealth but life', a philosophy which shines out from his vibrant paintings and drawings. Ruskin believed that everybody should be taught to draw as well as to read and write, and he was undoubtedly a good teacher. In this first room are some of his superb pencil sketches, including the hypnotic self-portrait of 1874. There are also some excellent watercolours such as *View from the Col de la Seigne*. Wildlife and the natural world feature strongly, as do Ruskin's curious and medieval-looking maps of the continents.

The work of Ruskin's secretary and friend, W.G. Collingwood, is represented in the next room by the superb *View of Yew Crag*. Ruskin spent some time abroad, particularly in Italy, researching architecture and its influence on the human condition, and producing his famous book *The Stones of Venice*, as well as many paintings and drawings. In this room we can see some examples. The pencil sketch of Pompeii is particularly fine, with a perspective that pulls us towards the very ruins themselves.

In the drawing room there is more Italian work as well as a shell collection and some 'Ruskin Linen' (see also the Ruskin Museum in Coniston, p. 88). Just off the drawing room is a smaller one lined with wall panels featuring a brief biography of the man. There are also some of his personal belongings – his coffee service, a chess set and a lock of his hair amongst others.

If you go back through the drawing room and turn right into the study you will find more drawings from *The Stones of Venice*, as well as shelves of rare books. The picture *Burial at Sea of Sir David Wilkie* by Isobella Jay may look vaguely familiar – it is a popular biscuit tin view. Notice also the wallpaper, recently reproduced from Ruskin's original design. Everywhere you are followed by Ruskin's eyes which look out from various photographs of the great man in old age.

Passing into the dining room you will see a bright and cheerful oil painting of Ruskin aged three, by James Northcote. The room is dominated by the dining table and other furniture, all originally brought in by Ruskin.

Upstairs you will find just two rooms open. On one side is the Turret Room, Ruskin's bedroom and his first addition to the house after taking it over. The other room contains a history of Brantwood in the 1890s.

Brantwood is an enigmatic place, and it is sometimes difficult to picture the man who was its most famous owner, but if you pause and study his paintings and sketches you can gain some understanding of the philosophy that drove him. In some respects he was ahead of his time – his predictions for the fate of the environment, made in the heat of the nineteenth-century industrial revolution, fell on deaf ears. There are echoes in this house that need to be heard again now.

Brantwood

Penrith and the Pennines

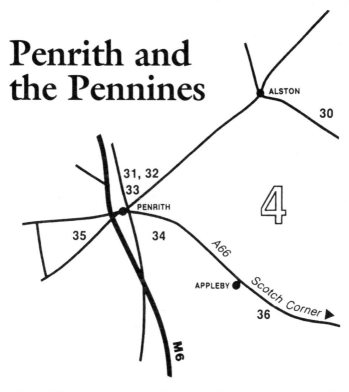

30 Killhope Wheel Lead Mining Centre, Stanhope *98*
31 Cumbria Police Museum, Penrith *101*
32 Penrith Town Museum *104*
33 Penrith Steam Museum *107*
34 Wetheriggs Country Pottery, Penrith *111*
35 Dalemain, Penrith *114*
36 Dyke Nook Farm, Appleby *117*

Killhope Wheel
Lead Mining Centre
Stanhope

Open April–October *Admission charge*

Hours 10.30–5.00, every day; 10.30–6.00 during August

Address Contact via Durham County Council, Countryside Team, County Hall, Durham DH1 5UQ

Telephone (0388) 537505

Suitability for children All ages, although some of the technology will need a little explaining.

Refreshments There are very good facilities on site.

Interest Mining history.

How to get there The centre is located in Upper Weardale alongside the A689 Stanhope to Alston road. (Alston is about 8 miles away, Barnard Castle about 29 miles.) Buses run regularly from Stanhope to Killhope, and on summer Sundays special trains connect at Stanhope with buses to and from Alston via Killhope.

Other attractions nearby South Tynedale Railway at Alston, other mining remains at Nenthead, and Bowes Museum at Barnard Castle.

The Killhope Lead Mining Centre is situated around the old entrance to Park Level Mine, which was last worked in 1916. The Park Level Mine entrance portal can still be seen, with an example of a typical horse-drawn mine tub outside it, just beyond the new Visitor Centre. Killhope is undergoing continuous development, with new exhibits opening up all the time.

The first building is the mineshop. Downstairs you will find the smithy, which is still in use. Here the blacksmith, the fitter of his day, repaired, made and improvised machinery to keep the mine working. Though he would have fitted some horseshoes, his main activity was sharpening tools for the miners.

Upstairs in the mineshop is the former office and some miners' lodgings. Many miners worked several miles from home and so stayed all week in a lodging shop like this one. They brought all their food with them in a 'wallet', one of the large linen bags you can see hanging over the beams in the room.

Life for the miners, even above ground, was generally unpleasant. The sleeping accommodation was overcrowded and dirty, and the smell must have been appalling. If the mine was very active then up to three men would have used one of the bunks with a boy stretched across at the foot. Clothes would have been hung up in front of the fire to dry and the harmful dust in them would drift around the airless room (in winter the windows were kept tight shut). Lung disease killed many miners in their early forties.

Beyond the mineshop are the washing floors and 'bouse-steads' where the ore was dumped ready for sorting and washing by 'bouseteams'. The 'teams' are the storage areas where each partnership of miners kept its hard-earned ore prior to washing. The various devices used to wash the ore are reconstructed here for you to have a go at. Washing and sorting the ore required copious quantities of water, in this case from the mine itself. In winter the conditions for the young boys who did the work were truly terrible. The Killhope washer boys went on strike in 1882, demanding a rise in their daily wage of ninepence. They didn't get it.

Beyond the washing floors is the crushing plant, built in the 1870s in response to increased ore production. The crushing was a fully mechanised operation, driven by the massive water-wheel that dominates the whole site. The Killhope Wheel is now the only surviving waterwheel connected with a North Pennines lead mining site. It contains 7,808 rivets, has 72 buckets, produced about 47 horsepower and used over 6,000 gallons of water a minute or 1,000 tons an hour! Beside the wheel are the remains of the massive rollers which pulverised the ore into walnut-sized lumps. These lumps were then fed into the jigger house where the ore itself was separated from the waste.

Returning past a small saddle house you have the option of taking a $\frac{3}{4}$-mile walk around the forest above the site where you can see some interesting reconstructions of early mining activity. The walk is well set out, with steps and wooden walkways to make the going easy.

There are also some reconstructions of sixteenth-century shallow shafts and an eighteenth-century horse gin (a type of winding gear). The descent back to the main site is by Hazely Hush, an apparently natural ravine, which is in fact entirely man-made. It was created, over time, by the release of vast quantities of water from further up the hill.

Killhope is a fascinating place, set high in the wild North Pennine hills, though the rather clean and tidy air of the modern site belies the awful working conditions suffered by the miners of 100 years ago. If you want to find out more about the site and the people who lived and worked here there is an excellent guidebook available from the museum shop.

Killhope wheel (courtesy of Durham County Council)

Cumbria Police Museum
Penrith

Open By appointment with the Curator *Admission free*

Address Cumbria Police Museum, Cumbria Constabulary, Carleton Hall, Penrith, Cumbria CA10 2AU

Telephone (0768) 64411 (Extension 7060)

Suitability for children Only accessible to school groups.

Refreshments There are several cafés and pubs in Penrith town centre, about 2 miles away.

Interest Police history and crime prevention.

How to get there The museum is just off the A686 Alston road, east out of Penrith. Limited parking is available for visitors. The nearest railway station is at Penrith, about 2 miles away.

Other attractions nearby Penrith Steam Museum (p.107), Dyke Nook Farm Museum (p.117) and Penrith Town Museum (p.104).

Located in the Cumbria Police Headquarters in Penrith, this museum reflects the history of the former County, Borough and City forces that now constitute the Cumbria Police. The room is split into two levels with a stage at one end.

On the left is an introductory section on the history of policing in Britain. The story begins with the 'Charlies' of 1663, old and infirm men who were armed with a bell, lantern and rattle. Needless to say they were of little use against determined robbers! In 1750 one Henry Fielding, a magistrate in Westminster, started the first detective force, Mr Fielding's People, later known as the 'Bow Street Runners'. The first true police force, the 'Peelers' or 'Bobbies', named after Sir Robert Peel, appeared after the 1829 Metropolitan Police Act.

A wall chart describes the history of the Cumbria police forces, starting in 1857 when the first chief Constable, Sir John Dunne, was appointed to cover the two counties of Cumberland

and Westmorland. Within three months he had established an effective force and introduced a system of training. He emphasised prevention rather than detection, and aimed to break down public prejudice by 'just and equitable rule'. On display here are a watch and chain presented to him by the Emperor of Germany.

The Police Museum (courtesy of Cumbria Constabulary)

Other display cabinets contain many items relating to nearly 150 years of policing in the area, including belt buckles, truncheons, handcuffs and whistles. A section on transport and communication shows some historic photographs, including one taken in 1913 of Chief Superintendent William Graham astride his horse. A police launch flag is proudly displayed, as well as some photographs of the various launches that have been used on the lakes over the years.

A large central case contains the dress uniform – cutlass, cocked hat, boots and jacket – of P.T.B. Browne, Chief Constable from 1926 to 1951. Alongside this is a rather gruesome display of assorted weapons and housebreaking tools retrieved from Cumbrian villains over the years.

Another wall chart tells the story of John Hatfield, a notorious conman, who bigamously married the famous beauty known as the Maid of Buttermere. In the nineteenth century murder was not the only capital offence. He was hanged for forgery on the sands outside Carlisle on 3 September 1803.

The museum also has a very interesting section on crime detection, with explanation of fingerprinting and analysis processes, using such exotic terms as the 'tented arch' and 'lateral pocket loop'. The reverse side of this display highlights one particular Cumbrian criminal case – the Netherby Hall Robbery of 1885. Three villains called Rudge, Martin and Baker had been touring the country committing crimes and using the railways as a means of escape. Under the cover of a popular coursing event at Longtown they raided nearby Netherby Hall at 8pm on 28 October, getting away with £250 worth of jewellery. Road blocks were set up and the robbers were challenged at Carlisle. A chase ensued, two officers were shot, the men were then spotted on the railway line south of the city. They didn't get far – Rudge and Martin were caught at Tebay, and Baker at Lancaster. They were all eventually hanged at Carlisle Gaol. On display here are the revolvers used in the robbery, a set of skeleton keys and a lantern used by the three men.

The main feature of this museum is a reconstruction of part of an early twentieth-century charge office, in which a distinctly evil-looking robber is being charged by the sergeant. A taped commentary adds drama to the scene.

The Cumbria Police Museum is a specialised museum devoted to one aspect of Cumbrian history, but as the museum leaflet states, 'the history of a police force is, in many respects, the history of the area and the society it serves'. It is well worth a look, but do bear in mind that it is only open by appointment and is therefore best visited as part of a group booking (you also get a tour of the control room included this way).

Penrith Town Museum
Penrith

Open All year *Admission free*

Hours June–September: Monday–Saturday, 10.00–7.00; Sunday, 10.00–6.00
October–May: 10.00–5.00 every day

Address Robinson's School, Middlegate, Penrith, Cumbria CA11 7PT

Telephone (0768) 64671 (Extension 228)

Suitability for children 10 years and above.

Refreshments There are several pubs and cafés in the nearby town centre.

Interest Local history, archaeology and geology.

How to get there The museum is located at the northern end of town. Street parking is available nearby or you can use the car parks near the bus station. There are good bus connections from Carlisle and other Cumbrian centres; the bus station in Sandgate is about five minutes walk away. Penrith railway station is about 10 minutes walk away.

Other attractions nearby Penrith Steam Museum (p. 107), Cumbria Police Museum (p. 101) and Wetheriggs Country Pottery (p. 111).

Penrith Museum is housed in the old Robinson's School, a building with a long history of its own. It was opened in 1670 as a charity school for 'the educating and bringing up of poore Gerles ... to read and Seamstry worke or such other Learning fitt for that sex'. The school was named after William Robinson, a wealthy grocer who made his fortune in London. In his will Robinson left £20 a year 'forever' to pay for the education of poor children. The building remained in use as a school for 300 years. Though this museum dates back to 1883, it only moved to Robinson's School in 1985, and a newly refurbished exhibition was opened by the actor/playwright Colin Welland in 1990.

You enter the museum through the Tourist Information Centre. There are two floors of exhibits and, following modern trends, considerable space is given over to temporary themed displays at different times of the year.

The ground floor has a central series of display cases containing some interesting items relating to local history. Multure dishes, for example, were used to take the toll payments in salt and corn from traders in the market. The brass dishes were used until 1880 when the toll was changed to a cash payment instead. There is the town crier's bell, and the old seal of Penrith which was rediscovered in a ditch near Brampton Church. You will also see some delightful miniature castings of woodworking and agricultural tools from a nearby iron foundry, and detailed descriptions of local industries.

Local characters are highlighted. Here are the cups, medals and belts of William Jameson, champion wrestler, along with a wonderful description of the man by a rather sceptical writer from the Pall Mall *Gazette*: 'more like a polar bear on its hind legs in a grey flannel shirt than a human being – huge as he is he was entered for the pole-vaulting and apparently proposed to throw his huge hillock of flesh some 9 to 10 feet into the air!'

Trooper William Pearson was also something of a local hero. A veteran of the Charge of the Light Brigade in 1854, Pearson was amongst the 195 men, out of 600, who returned from the 'Valley of Death' on that fateful day. He did not survive unscathed though – he was wounded in the shoulder and lost four toes to frostbite in the bitter winter that followed the battle. His campaign medals are displayed, as well as descriptions of the various campaigns.

On a gentler note an oil painting by Jacob Johnston, entitled *Downfall of Pride* (1864), depicts the consequences of the *Height of Ambition,* shown in a companion painting. Both works make their moral points against a background of impressive Lakeland scenery. A 'Cabinet of Curiosities' contains a motley collection of pottery, bottles, minerals, weapons and butterflies.

Beyond this first room is a temporary exhibition gallery and stairs up to the first floor. These stairs lead into another temporary exhibition gallery, after which you reach the archaeology and geology room. Here there are some finds from the Roman fort at Plumpton, including some red gloss Samian ware pottery. The prehistoric period is represented by some stone axes and, more interestingly, two fragments of 'cup and rings' marked stone from Maughanby which are about 4,000 years old. These curious markings are thought to have links with fertility rites.

The small but effective geology display takes us through the history of the Eden Valley from 450 million years ago. Then it was a shallow sea full of Trilobites (the overgrown woodlouse-like creatures) and the planktonic Graptolites. Around 290 million years ago the area became swampy forest populated with ferns and huge trees. Then, a mere 250 million years ago, it changed again to dry desert, and the dunes that now form the characteristic red sandstone of the area were deposited. There is a tantalising glimpse of one of the inhabitants from that time in the form of a reptilian footprint, made by a forerunner of the dinosaurs. The effects of glaciation are also described, effects still to be clearly seen in the landscape around Penrith.

Penrith Museum epitomises the best in small local museums, possessing a long history and some important collections. The new policy of temporary exhibitions enables much more of the varied history of the area to be presented at any one time.

Engraved wood and brass busk, used to stiffen ladies' corsets (courtesy of Eden District Council)

Penrith Steam Museum
Penrith

Open Easter Weekend, then Spring Bank Holiday–September
Admission charge

Hours 10.00–4.30, Monday–Friday and Bank Holiday weekends

Address Castlegate, Penrith, Cumbria

Telephone (0768) 62154

Suitability for children All ages.

Refreshments The small museum cafe is open intermittently; otherwise there are cafes in the nearby town centre.

Interest Steam engines, agricultural machinery and local history.

How to get there The museum is five minutes walk from the railway station, towards the town centre. There are pay and display car parks nearby.

Other attractions nearby Penrith Town Museum (p. 104), Cumbria Police Museum (p. 101) and Dalemain (p. 114).

The Penrith Steam Museum, one of Cumbria's undiscovered treasures, is very much a working museum, where you can watch blacksmiths and machine-shop workers produce farm implements and machinery. Located in a foundry previously owned by the firm of Stalker Brothers, the museum also specialises in steam engine restoration.

On entering you first pass through a small shop and then out into a spacious courtyard area. In the building to your left the ground floor has some old (and not so old) motorbikes: the Yamaha TR2B of 1971, and the rare DMW Hornet of 1965, powered by a Villiers 250cc Starmaker engine, are just two examples. (You will find more motorbikes gathered in a room at the end of the upstairs gallery.)

The next room on the ground floor contains models and various bits of steam machinery. There are some fine examples

107

of model steam engines, including steam wagons, fairground engines and a delightful scale model of a Burrell traction engine. At the far end is a reconstruction of an ironworks 'shop', where all types of cast iron products – stoves, boilers, presses, a weightstand and numerous cogs – are seen as though for sale. The centre of the room is occupied by some full-sized stationary steam engines, including a Witte drag saw, an evil-looking device used to cut up large logs.

Upstairs you will find a real curiosity. At first sight the room seems to be full of cast iron products from the former foundry, but in reality all the objects are made from wood! They were carefully carved by skilled pattern-makers to be used as moulds for the final cast iron products. Here are to be found road grids, railway 'chairs', yet more cogs and even the ornate carved finials from the top of old road signs. Beyond can be seen various items of agricultural machinery made by Stalkers, as well as a case of pattern-maker's woodworking tools. Up a couple of steps are more machines, such as a knife grinder's wheel, and a display of wooden letters, probably used in making cast iron road signs.

Retracing your steps back down to the courtyard, you can then turn left into a reconstructed Victorian town cottage. There is an impressive kitchen range (another Penrith product) and, opposite that, a small foot-powered organ, on which many a Victorian hymn was no doubt played with great gusto.

Back outside, there is the hiss of steam and a gentle whirring noise from the other side of the yard. This is *Robey*, a semi-portable, wood-fired, stationary engine, lovingly kept in working order. *Robey* would originally have been used for driving machinery out in the forests of Northumberland.

Next to *Robey*'s shed are the original foundry workshops where you can see craftsmen using the forge or one of the huge lathes. The bulk of the machinery dates back to the 1920s when the machine-shop was created to repair steam traction engines (then to be found on many farms throughout Cumberland and Westmorland).

Through the workshop and into the main museum gallery, you are greeted by a whole row of brightly polished road and traction engines. They include such delights as a Fowler road roller, *Little Jim* (a Mann Patent Steam Cart and Waggon Co product) and *Anne* (built by Garret and Son). In the centre is a bright blue Foden steam wagon painted in the colours of Jenning's Brewery in Cockermouth. The dominant feature, however, is the huge mill engine, named *Judith Hannah*, built by Pollitt and Wiggell Ltd in 1916 and originally located at Edmund Sykes & Sons Krumlin Mill in Halifax. A distinct curiosity is the Spensers Silverlite Generator. I looked very closely at the description but still couldn't work out what it did!

The walls of the gallery are lined with photographs of steam traction engines, including some shots of unfortunate accidents. (The weight of these engines often led to spectacular and sudden collapses of roads and bridges!) There is a small model railway in operation too.

Another display of photographs in the museum depicts the history of the firm of Stalker Brothers, the previous owners of the foundry. Stalker Brothers were recognised as experts on boilers and had developed a thriving business repairing and maintaining steam engines. The firm was founded in 1851 by Jonathan Stalker who had set himself up as a master blacksmith in Castlegate, making ploughs and other farm implements, many of which won prizes all over the north of England. The business soon developed into steam engine repair and maintenance and it was his grandson who finally sold the foundry to the new museum. All this history provides a wonderful atmosphere as you walk around the site.

The Penrith Steam Museum studiously avoids the limelight but is nevertheless a real star. It is truly a living museum, and some of its exhibits literally take to the roads at weekends during the summer months, visiting 'steam gatherings' all over the country.

Wetheriggs
Country Pottery
Penrith

Open All year *Admission charge*

Hours 10.00–6.00, every day.

Address Clifton Dykes, Penrith, Cumbria CA10 2DH

Telephone (0768) 62946

Suitability for children All ages.

Refreshments There is an excellent coffee shop on site.

Interest Industrial history and local pottery.

How to get there The pottery is signposted off the A6 south of Penrith, just beyond Eamont Bridge, and there is good parking on site. The nearest railway station is at Penrith, about four miles away.

Other attractions nearby Penrith Town Museum (p. 104), Penrith Steam Museum (p. 107) and Dyke Nook Farm Museum (p. 117). There is also a fascinating prehistoric monument, a henge, at Eamont Bridge, alongside the road to Pooley Bridge, just before the motorway crossing.

Now scheduled as an ancient monument, Wetheriggs Country Pottery began life as a brickworks and tilery in 1855. It was originally built for the estate of Brougham and Vaux, and was constructed alongside the old Eden Valley branch of the North Eastern Railway. Coal was supplied by train from the Cumbrian coalfields and the underlying boulder clay of the area provided the raw material for the works. The pottery developed from the brickworks in about 1865.

Eventually the combined effects of the new motorway and increased wages led to the pottery's decline in the early 1970s. However the new owners saw the opportunity to develop the site as a craft venue, concentrating on attracting the passing visitor trade. Since then another change of ownership has returned the pottery to something of its old ways, producing practical earthenware pottery in the traditional style.

What can you see when you visit? The main entrance is concealed within a large combined pottery shop and tea room. It's tempting to linger here but I would recommend a tour around the pottery first in order to gain an understanding of the historical processes that have led to the creation of the pots you can buy today.

If you bypass the buildings and walk around the far end of the site you will see the settling pans. After being churned up with water in the delightfully named blunger the raw clay formed a thin slurry which was fed down into these settling pans. Here it was left while the water evaporated, following which the clay was cut up into blocks and stored before use.

Today the clay is mixed by a pug mill which can be seen oozing out clay ready to be used by the potter. In the old days the processing machinery, including the blunger, was driven by a steam engine which can still be seen, along with its boiler, patiently awaiting restoration. The modern pottery machinery is driven by an extremely noisy but powerful diesel engine which looks as though it has come from the engine room of an ocean liner! If you fancy trying your hand at throwing a pot some wheels and clay are provided.

There is no doubt that the heart of the pottery is the old beehive kiln. Today it serves as a museum, full of examples of the different varieties of pottery that used to be made on site. Wetheriggs also used to produce many types of moulded wares, and the ornate Victorian moulds are to be found on display here. (They were made in a 'jolly shop' – a small building nearby – separated from the throwing room in order to avoid getting plaster in the clay.)

Today the pots are fired in efficient electric or gas kilns, but in the old days the massive beehive kiln was used. It could take up to 7,000 individual pieces of pottery at one go, and getting it up to temperature was no picnic! A complete firing took 6 tons of coal and 36 hours, with the eight fireboxes needing constant attention to maintain the temperature. There are plans to bring this wonderful dragon back to life on special occasions. It will be well worth waiting for.

Beehive kiln

Adjacent to the kiln is the pottery workshop. The room seems mysteriously warm, until you realise that the drying racks have a small fire feeding them at one end (rather like a Roman hypocaust). This not only keeps the place habitable in winter but also serves as a cosy retreat for numerous cats who can be found curled up inside some of the pots.

Wetheriggs is one of the few old country potteries that is still in active service. Most of our modern tableware is either made in another part of the world or is mass-produced in large factories in the Midlands. The results may be eminently usable, but they can hardly be said to have character. In their day potteries such as Wetheriggs produced some of the finest English slipwares, items that are still very highly prized.

This site has been recognised by government historians as a fine example of an industrial process representing an era now long gone (until the oil runs out, that is). Like Stott Park Bobbin Mill (p. 121) and the various water mills, it gives us a glimpse into the past, a past when tourism had not yet become the major industry in Cumbria.

Dalemain
Penrith

Open April–October *Admission charge*

Hours 11.15–5.00, Sunday–Thursday

Address Dacre, Penrith, Cumbria CA11 0HB

Telephone (07684) 86450

Suitability for children 10 years and above.

Refreshments There is a good tea room in the main house.

Interest Military, agricultural and natural history.

How to get there Dalemain is on the A592 west of Penrith, on the way to Ullswater. The nearest railway station is at Penrith.

Other attractions nearby Penrith Steam Museum (p. 107), Penrith Town Museum (p. 104) and Ullswater Lake Steamers.

Dalemain has been described as the finest historic house in the northern Lakes. However, since I don't have room to include historic houses in this Guide, you will have to venture inside to test this claim for yourself. Here I shall concentrate on the three museums to be found in and around the main house and courtyard.

Out in the courtyard area and up some stone steps can be found the Countryside and Bird Museum, a strange mixture of stuffed birds, eggs, shells and items such as shotgun cartridge-making equipment. Few older taxidermy displays in museums are without some natural monstrosity, and here we have the four-legged chick! More conventionally, there are spectacular species such as a golden eagle and a mountain hare. The rather gruesome shooting ephemera is supplemented by various animal traps hanging on the wall. These items were once the main way of controlling pests, whereas today we use poisons and chemicals which may seem less cruel but probably do more damage to the environment in the long run.

Another collection is to be found across the yard in a sixteenth-century barn. The Fell Pony Museum concentrates on this ancient breed's contribution to the local economy. In their day these hardy little beasts were to be found at work both above and below ground. As evidence of their underground activity there is a pit-tub and harness from a mine in Northumberland, along with an ambulance trolley used to haul injured miners to the foot of the mine shafts.

In the corner of the gallery is a reconstructed blacksmith's forge where the ponies were shod. A saddler's shop, originally from Greenodd in the south of the County, has also been rebuilt. The items in it were carefully preserved for 17 years after the shop closed down. You will see the prize rosettes carefully laid out, along with the 'calling cards' used to advertise the services of various prize stallions! Elsewhere are some agricultural exhibits relating to life on an estate such as Dalemain.

The third museum is to be found in the base of the old Norman pele tower which was originally built as a stronghold against the Scots and other likely marauders. This museum concentrates on the history of the Westmorland and Cumberland Yeomanry, as well as the two volunteer forces that preceded it – the Westmorland East and West Wards Local Militia and the Cumberland Loyal Leath Ward Volunteers.

The Yeomanry Cavalry Regiment was first raised in 1819 by Edward Hasell (an ancestor of the present owners of Dalemain), and he was to remain its Colonel for 50 years. Training camps were held each summer, often at Lowther Park nearby, and photographs of these colourful events are on display.

A company of cavalry saw action in the Boer War, and during the First World War the Yeomanry became divisional cavalry, seeing action at Gallipoli and in France. Soon one battalion became a cyclist brigade and others were dismounted and attached to infantry units.

The Yeomanry was a force made up of neighbours and friends, all from the same district, all sharing a sense of comradeship and a feeling for tradition and loyalty. Something of that pride comes out in these displays. You will see a black field dress tunic worn by Major John Hasell, and some resplendent red dress uniforms. Undress 'Shako' caps are offset by an ornate full dress version, complete with plume. Swords and spurs remind us of the cavalry tradition and there are photographs of troopers both at rest and on exercises which seem to have included use of the Windermere ferry!

Among a number of interesting items is the set of original designs for the flag of the Loyal Leath Ward Volunteers. A box of numbered blocks was used to instruct cavalry troopers in the rudiments of manoeuvres, and the fine silver cup on display was presented to Edward Hasell, Colonel Commandant in 1811, by the East and West Ward Militia. There are also orderly books dating back to the mid-nineteenth century.

Perhaps the most poignant items on display are the original call-up telegrams sent out to the Yeomanry on 4/5 August 1914. This was to be no summer exercise; it was the culmination of all the training and effort that had occupied these men for so many years. Yet, in the space of a few short months in late 1914, the face of war was to change forever. The glory of the cavalry charge was to be replaced by the perpetual hell of trench warfare, and the Yeomanry was finally disbanded after the war ended.

Having been around the museums, do take time to look at the rest of the house and gardens. The guidebook and tea rooms are recommended. The house retains much of the atmosphere of a family home, with a delightful room devoted to children's toys being a particular attraction. The gardens are intimate and well stocked, and in summer events such as craft fairs are held here.

Dyke Nook Farm Museum
Appleby

Open July–August *Admission charge*

Hours 1.00–5.00, every day except Thursday and Saturday

Address Dyke Nook, Warcop, nr Appleby, Cumbria

Telephone (07683) 41207

Suitability for children 10 years and above.

Refreshments There is a selection of places in Appleby.

Interest Agricultural machinery.

How to get there Dyke Nook is signposted off the A66 about 4 miles east of Appleby, and there is parking on site. The nearest railway station is at Appleby on the Settle to Carlisle line, but buses from there are infrequent.

Other attractions nearby Brough Castle (owned by English Heritage) and the Settle to Carlisle scenic railway.

This type of small agricultural collection is something of a rarity in Cumbria where, surprisingly for such a rural county, there are few places where you can see the wide variety of tools and equipment associated with farming. Here, however, is an amazing collection of mechanised labour-savers, ranging from large threshing machines to poultry incubators.

Most of the collection is housed in a large modern building and laid out with just enough space for you to wander round. There is no apparent order to the display – just pick out objects at random for closer examination. The stitch harrow, for example, was apparently used for knocking out the weeds between stitches (this explanation probably makes more sense if you are from a farming background!). There are root cutters, chaff cutters, seed drills (used for popping seeds into prepared ground), and even some Humbug pliers (not what you might think – they were used for restraining cattle by the nose).

Potato planters jostle against box mangles, dolly legs (a sort of manual Hotpoint) and large colourful horse-drawn wagons. The vast array of items displayed may give you visual overload. It's rather like looking at an industrial collection from the biggest factory in the world – the soil itself. The ways in which human beings have avoided using their hands whilst labouring on the land are truly breathtaking in their ingenuity.

The production end of the dairy farming process is represented by milking machinery and a large double cheese press, tremendous pressure being needed to compress the raw material into the final product. In one corner is a stationary engine curiously bearing a University of Leeds Mechanical Engineering Department plate. What on earth did they use it for? A Fordson tractor lurks in another corner wearing a pair of heavily spiked rear wheels, presumably for traversing heavy clay soils.

By now you may wish to retire from all this mechanical confusion. Outside there are some interesting exhibits, including a delightful four-wheeled 'gypsy caravan', complete with stove bunk and numerous cupboards. The curved roof appears to be insulated with carpet! The most attractive outdoor item, though, has to be *Margaret,* all 8.5 tons of her. She is a traction engine built by J.H McLaren of Leeds.

And now onwards and upstairs to a space devoted to some more agricultural and rural curiosities. Domestic items – such as a haybox cooker, various types of iron, and an early vacuum (still in its box) – can be seen, and there are some treadle sewing machines and a whole row of clogs. Recent history is represented by a gas mask and a small child's bicycle made in 1940. The list of exhibits is endless (don't miss the ferret box!) and it's a bit like looking round a large antique shop. Many museums tend to put over-long, wordy labels with their exhibits. Here the opposite is true – but at least it allows your imagination free rein. It's a wonderful place for children to ask their parents awkward questions about strange bits of machinery. As Dyke Nook is a working farm they will also enjoy looking at the animals.

This museum is a curious place, full of wonderfully mysterious objects. The ingenuity of design that went into this machinery is worth taking time to consider. Indeed, this sort of intermediate technology may not yet have outlived its usefulness.

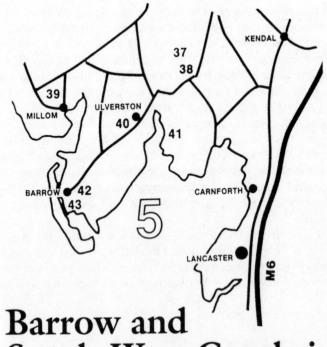

Barrow and South-West Cumbria

37 Stott Park Bobbin Mill, Finsthwaite *121*
38 Lakeside and Haverthwaite Railway *123*
39 Millom Folk Museum *125*
40 Laurel and Hardy Museum, Ulverston *128*
41 Lakeland Motor Museum, Holker Hall *130*
42 Furness Museum, Barrow-in-Furness *134*
43 The Dock, Barrow-in-Furness *136*

Stott Park Bobbin Mill
Finsthwaite

Open Easter–October *Admission charge*

Hours 10.00–6.00, every day

Address Stott Park Bobbin Mill, Finsthwaite, Newby Bridge, Cumbria

Telephone (05395) 31087

Suitability for children 10 years and above.

Refreshments Available nearby at the Lakeside ferry terminal.

Interest Industrial archaeology and social history.

How to get there Located on the west side of Windermere, the mill is signposted on the road between Lakeside and Hawkshead. There is parking at the mill. The nearest railway station is at Windermere, with a ferry from there to Lakeside. It's about a mile to the museum from there.

Other attractions nearby Lakeside and Haverthwaite Railway (p. 123) and Windermere Steamboat Museum (p. 91).

This is one of the last working examples of the ancient woodland industries that used to be found all over the Lake District. Unlike charcoal-burning and potash pits, though, bobbin-making could be mechanised.

Originally, crude treadle lathes were operated by foot. This method was soon superseded by a waterwheel approximately 32 feet in diameter and advertised at the time as 'equal to sixteen horses' power'. It drove a veritable 'cat's cradle' of pulleys which in turn powered the individual lathes and other machines. However during dry periods the machines and men had to stand idle. The wheel was therefore replaced by a water turbine in the mid-nineteenth century, then supplemented by a steam engine in the 1890s. The turbine was eventually replaced by an electric motor in the 1940s.

The production line was geared to process the raw material – debarked coppice poles – into sawn lengths, then into bored cylinders and 'roughs', and then into the final product, smooth polished bobbins for use in the cotton and other textile industries. It was not just bobbins that were, literally, turned out – yoyos, skipping rope handles, toy wheels, and toggles for Royal Navy duffle coats were just some of the other products made here.

At Stott Park you are led through the complete process of making bobbins. The speed of operation is truly breathtaking – who would have thought that all this effort went into making the humble cotton reel! It was a remarkably self-sufficient industry: water was freely available (as it always is in the Lake District), coppice woods were developed close by, and the offcuts and wood shavings were even used to fuel the steam engine boiler.

Stott Park does not have displays in glass cases; it is a living museum devoted to an industry now almost gone from the region. The Victorian buildings have been carefully restored and give a fascinating insight not only into the manufacture of bobbins but also into the local economy, the industrial revolution, and Victorian engineering and inventiveness.

The Lakeside and Haverthwaite Railway
Haverthwaite

Open Easter–November *Admission charge (for trains)*

Hours Train times vary with the season – phone for details.

Address Haverthwaite Station, Near Ulverston, Cumbria
LA12 8AL

Telephone (05395) 31594

Suitability for children All ages.

Refreshments There is an excellent restaurant in the Haverthwaite
station building.

Interest Steam trains and nostalgia.

How to get there Haverthwaite station is just off the A590 near
Newby Bridge and there is good parking on site. The nearest British
Rail stations are at Ulverston and Windermere, and buses pass to
and from Ulverston.

Other attractions nearby Holker Hall and Lakeland Motor
Museum (p. 130), Lake Windermere cruises, and Windermere
Steamboat Museum (p. 91)

One of the three operating steam railways in Cumbria (the
Ravenglass and Eskdale and the South Tynedale Railway are
the other two), the Lakeside and Haverthwaite Railway was
originally a branch of the Furness Railway, carrying passengers
to and from Lakeside. However when the adjacent A590 was
realigned the railway was severed from the rest of the main rail
network. Undeterred, a dedicated band of enthusiasts have
created an active steam railway that now runs for $3\frac{1}{2}$ miles from
Haverthwaite, through some particularly attractive scenery, to
Lakeside on Windermere. Connections can be made at Lakeside
for trips on the superb Windermere Steamboat Company vessels

which ply the 10-mile length of the lake.

Although not officially designated as a museum, the railway engine sheds and workshops contain some interesting items, most of which are accessible to the visitor. During the season you may see one or more of a number of steam locomotives in action. Look out for *Cumbria*, an 0–6–0 saddle tank built by Hunslet in 1953, and *Repulse*, a similar engine, both of which tend to handle most of the daily passenger traffic.

Inside the main shed you first come across a scale model of Haverthwaite station as it would have looked around 1923. There is a surprise here too: a Royal coach, Princess Alexandra's saloon, built by the Great Eastern Railway in 1898, which now reluctantly rubs shoulders with a rather unrefined-looking LMS (London Midland and Scottish) guards van of 1944!

There are also various diesel locomotives. *Rachel* is one example, a curious industrial shunting loco of 1924 which came from Croppers Paper Mill. Continuity of design is represented by two very similar diesel shunting locos: one built by the old LMS in 1945; the other by BR in 1959. Local colour is added by *David*, an 0–4–0 saddle tank from the Millom Ironworks. There are some larger engines too – a Fairburn design class 4MT tank engine, built in 1951, and a similar locomotive lying mostly in bits awaiting funds for restoration.

Now isolated from the rest of the rail system, the Lakeside and Haverthwaite Railway has developed an atmosphere all its own. A visit here is perhaps best combined with a voyage on Lake Windermere. This involves travelling from Haverthwaite to Lakeside and then joining a ferry there for a return trip on the lake.

Lakeside Station is a small but vibrant hive of activity with its roots firmly planted in the past. The dedication of this little railway's supporters has ensured that it stands every chance of being as successful as its ancestor, the Furness Railway.

Millom Folk Museum
Millom

Open May–September *Admission charge*

Hours 10.00–5.00, every day except Sunday

Address St George's Road, Millom, Cumbria LA18 4DD

Telephone (0229) 772555

Suitability for children All ages.

Refreshments Available close by in the town centre.

Interest Local history and industrial history.

How to get there The nearest railway station is about five minutes walk away. There is parking in the town square nearby.

Other attractions nearby Furness Museum (p. 134) and Ravenglass and Eskdale Railway (p. 61).

Millom Folk Museum has the only collection of material from the once famous local iron industry. This delightful museum, which is the result of many years of dedicated collecting by an enthusiastic band of local people, also serves as the local Tourist Information Centre. Housed in a former school, its displays occupy just about every available corner. The volunteers have also reconstructed a full-size 'drift' (tunnel) from the local iron mine, complete with a mine cage from the Moorbank Shaft.

It was the closure of the Hodbarrow Mines in 1968 that inspired the local people to make a start on preserving and interpreting their historic past before it was bulldozed forever. Millom's rich iron ore deposits were first exploited by Cornishmen in the 1850s. They and their successors eventually extracted over 28 million tons of the richest iron ore to be found anywhere in the world. At the peak of its success Hodbarrow paid dividends to its shareholders every two weeks.

The museum has a substantial display of items relating to these mines, including many historic photographs of the massive breakwaters built to try and keep the sea out of the mine workings. You can still see the sad remains of these major works of civil engineering. Samples of the much-prized haematite, also known as 'kidney ore', are on display, as well as detonator boxes and mine survey equipment. One curiosity is the Millom Skull, a fragment of human skull found buried deep below the surface when some old workings collapsed. Is it from a prehistoric inhabitant or some unfortunate miner who died more recently?

Iron ore was not only mined at Millom, it was processed here as well – the massive Millom Ironworks produced high-quality steel. Life in the town revolved around the iron industry and whole streets were built by the company to house their workers. These terraced rows sometimes had less than imaginative names – Steel Green Terrace and Concrete Square are two examples (now demolished).

Millom isn't all steel though – there was a maritime influence here too. Pictures show some of the vessels built in the vicinity, such as the West Coast ketch the *Emily Barret*, which can be seen nearby at the Dock, Barrow-in-Furness (p. 136). There are some photographs of the wrecked *Coniston* of 1917 on display as well, and a stretcher used to remove bodies from the seashore.

Amongst the farming and domestic displays is a small recon-struction of a blacksmith's forge and a whole array of other agricultural items. I'm not quite sure where the 100-year-old hot cross bun fits in, but it certainly seems to have a home here! One of Millom's most famous inhabitants was Norman Nicholson, the renowned poet and author. There is a certain reverence attached to the displays devoted to him. He actually opened the museum in 1973 and was taught in the very room that it now occupies.

Going round the corner to a smaller gallery, you can pause to see the Hodbarrow mine reconstruction, which, considering the restricted space, is very well done. All it lacks is the cold clammy atmosphere (although I'm sure the museum volunteers would suggest a visit here in winter to rectify this!). Beyond is a beautifully reconstructed miner's cottage interior, done with great attention to detail, even including some hot pot on the table. You can also see a very realistic old shop setting. The window contains all sorts of items, from toys to old grocer's bags.

Millom Folk Museum is a truly local museum. It is a community effort in every sense of the word, demonstrating a pride in its history that has survived the trauma of losing the town's major industry. The 'red men' of Millom may have gone but their past lives on through the varied displays and collections to be seen here.

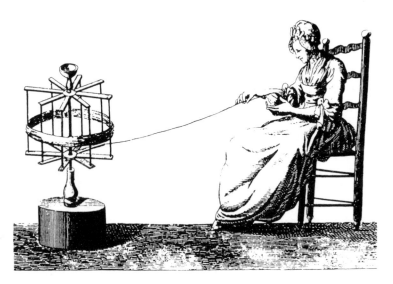

Laurel and Hardy Museum
Ulverston

Open All year *Admission charge*

Hours 10.00–4.30, every day

Address 4C Upper Brook Street, Ulverston, Cumbria LA12 7BH

Telephone (0229) 52292

Suitability for children All ages.

Refreshments There are several cafés nearby.

Interest Pure film nostalgia.

How to get there Travel into Ulverston on the A590 then turn into town at the traffic lights on Queen Street. There is parking in Mill Street and Daltongate. Ulverston is well served by buses, and the railway station is about 10 minutes walk away for trains on the Lancaster to Barrow line.

Other attractions nearby The Coronation Hall sometimes has interesting temporary exhibitions. If you feel like a good walk then try Hoad Hill and its landlocked lighthouse. The Cumbria Crystal workshops are in Lightburn Road.

This has to be one of the funniest museums in the County. It's not only a museum but a 1920s cinema as well, showing silent footage of Laurel and Hardy films. Why is this museum to be found here in Cumbria? Because Stan Laurel, one of its more famous sons, was born at No. 3 Argyle Street, Ulverston, on 16 June 1890.

Bull Cubin, owner, curator, projectionist and Grand Sheik of the Ulverston Birthmark's Tent of the Sons of the Desert (the Laurel and Hardy fan club) proudly displays his large collection of memorabilia featuring the famous duo. He started the museum in 1976 and finally got planning permission for it seven years later!

On entering the dimly lit ground floor room, tucked away

off Upper Brook Street, the visitor first becomes aware of the rows of seats (originally from a cinema in Accrington and of 1928 vintage). Here you can linger to watch as many of the old Laurel and Hardy films as you can digest at one sitting. Off to the right (through a door Bill knocked through in 1981) is another room – or perhaps shrine is a better description – filled with every imaginable bit of Stan Laurel and Oliver Hardy memorabilia. Pride of place is taken by three treasured objects: a heartfelt fan letter to Stan Laurel from a five-year-old boy; an ashtray from Stan's home in Santa Monica, California; and Stan's father's silver cigarette case (presented to him on his retirement in 1925 by the staff of the Eden Theatre, Bishop Auckland, where he was manager).

Apart from these items the visitor is confronted with wall-to-wall nostalgia: the walls are literally covered with pictures, newspaper cuttings and film posters. There are also souvenir items to be bought in Bill's small museum shop. Rarely do you find a curator as enthusiastic about his collection as Bill Cubin. If you enjoy silent films and share Bill's dedication to the memory of the silver screen's most famous duo then be prepared for a long stay!

Lakeland Motor Museum, Holker Hall
Cark-in-Cartmel

Open April–October *Admission charge*

Hours 10.30–4.30, every day

Address Holker Hall, Cark-in-Cartmel, Grange-over-Sands, Cumbria LA11 7PL

Telephone (05395) 58509

Suitability for children All ages.

Refreshments There are tea rooms in the adjacent buildings.

Interest Motor vehicle history, technology and nostalgia.

How to get there Holker Hall is signposted off the A590 Barrow road, about 5 miles from Grange, and there is good parking on site. The nearest railway station is at Cark, about 15 minutes walk away.

Other attractions nearby Lakeside and Haverthwaite Railway (p. 123), Grizedale Forest Park, and the Laurel and Hardy Museum (p. 128).

Situated in the grounds of historic Holker Hall, the Lakeland Motor Museum is a celebration of the motor car in all its forms, but also includes an excellent bicycle display and some vintage motorbikes.

Having passed through the well-stocked shop, you will first see some early motorbikes, including a 1930 Royal Ruby believed to be the only one now in existence. There is the superb Matchless G12 of 1960, winner of the 'Jampot' Concours d'Elegance in 1982; and the 1950 Corgi Scooter, the civilian version of the military 'Welbike' which was designed to fold up and fit into a special container for parachute drops.

Amongst the cars in the first section is a 1923 Wolseley two-seater and a 1929 Fiat 509A. (Over 90,000 of these Fiats were sold in Italy at a time when only 172,000 private cars were registered there.) The delightful Morris 8 family saloon must be one of the few cars that actually dropped in price as production increased, from £175 to £125, in direct competition with the Austin 7 range.

Bicycles feature here too, and there are some fine examples to be seen, particularly the Rudge Rotary Tricycle of 1885. Nestling amongst them when I visited was *Matilda,* the 1923 Jowett 7/17 Coupé, which has never been off the road since it was built and has won many trials.

In the corner of the main gallery are two much larger vehicles, a Dennis Fire engine of 1914 and a 1947 KZ ambulance. The Dennis engine, originally supplied to the Wimbledon Fire Brigade in 1914, has been fully restored by the present Dennis Company apprentices. It has a White and Poppe engine, solid tyres, a brass bell, bulb horn and hoses. The ambulance, fully restored inside and out, is something of a star, having recently featured in the Granada TV production *Spoils of War,* which was filmed at Millom in south-west Cumbria. Elegance in travel is represented by the Cadillac Fleetwood limousine, a classic American automobile. It has a massive V8 engine and only does 12 miles to the gallon. It was always chauffeur-driven and is consequently in immaculate condition.

If you now take a breather from the cars themselves and look around the walls you will see some real curiosities – number plates from all over the world, and a fascinating display of bonnet mascots, including elegant 'lithe spirits', the bulbous 'Michelin Man', and some calormeters which incorporated a temperature gauge in the radiator cap.

Going back to the cars, you will come across a 1929 Essex Super Six, with its 2.1 litre six-cylinder engine. Over 300,000 of these cars were sold in 1929 – 6.6 per cent of the total American registration. It was to prove equally popular in Britain, mainly because of its multi-cylinder engine. My own favourite is the Lagonda Drop Head Coupé, with its V12 4480 cc engine which gave an acceleration of 0–50 in 10 seconds, and a top speed of 100 mph. Something rather less exotic but with Royal connections is the plain little Vespa Sportique. It was bought by Princess Margaret in 1964 – and the registration document is here to prove it.

There are more cabinet displays here, including a whole range of coloured glass Avon scent bottles moulded in all sorts of shapes connected with cars and trains. Another display highlights the slow introduction of electric bulbs in cars. Most early lamps were oil (for side and tail) or acetylene (for headlights).

One of the most curious exhibits is the distinctly inelegant DMW Amphicar of 1965. The only amphibious private car on the world market, it had two propellers mounted under the back driven by special gears, and was powered by a 1200 cc Triumph engine. On the road the car was capable of about 70 mph, on water about 7 knots! The normal steering was used afloat; presumably fairly successfully, for in 1962 an Amphicar crossed the English Channel.

The sporting end of the market is represented by some successful and some not so successful vehicles. The 1951 Lotus, the first racing car ever built by Colin Chapman, is a superb example of the former. It is a hill-climbing aluminium-bodied special, based on the Austin 7 but with a top speed of 100 mph rather than the 45 mph of the normal model. The ill-fated De Lorean was built in Northern Ireland in a brave attempt to provide both employment and a new sports car for the British market, but soon ran into financial problems. The plant was closed down, and today the only De Lorean you are likely to see is on the TV screen, in futuristic sci-fi movies.

And so the displays continue. There are some early arcade games for you to try in one of the galleries – most have a motoring theme and are a welcome change from the video computer-games of today. Children might also be interested in the various toy pedal cars in the collection. My choice would be the Austin J40, built from scrap panels on the Longbridge production lines. Over 32,000 of these marvellous toys were made before production ceased in 1971.

Two of the most intriguing exhibits are also the most recent acquisitions. The Africar was the result of one man's dream –

to design a car that the Third World could build and maintain itself. The project was supported by Channel 4 Television and it featured in a TV documentary series in the early 1980s. The museum bought this example when the factory, sadly, failed a couple of years ago. The other newcomer is the appalling Trabant, the 'people's car' from East Germany (as was). It has a body made from pressed paper and resin and the petrol tank is in the engine compartment!

The most visually stimulating displays are set out in a reconstructed 1930s garage. Here are all the tools, spares and timeless junk associated with any garage through the ages. It's worth lingering to see how many items you recognise from your own garage.

The Lakeland Motor Museum has a superb collection of automotive memorabilia, with something for all the family to enjoy. In fact Holker requires almost a whole day to take in, for there are other collections on site, including the excellent Countryside Museum (which covers local natural history), as well as farm animals and an adventure playground.

The Furness Museum and the Dock
Barrow-in-Furness

Furness Museum

Note At the time of going to press the future of this museum was under review and a new location was being considered. Please check with the Tourist Information Office before making your visit.

Address Ramsden Square, Barrow-in-Furness, Cumbria LA14 1LL

Telephone (0229) 820650

Refreshments Available at Forum 28 (Arts Centre) about 10 minutes walk towards the Town Hall.

Suitability for children 10 years and above.

Interest Local history.

How to get there See note above.

Other attractions nearby Marine activity around the Vickers shipyard, and Furness Abbey (owned by English Heritage).

The Furness Museum occupies (at the time of writing) a room above Barrow Library next to the County Archives Office – a fitting place to tell the story of the town through a variety of interesting objects.

At the top of the stairs you will find a small lobby area used for temporary exhibitions. There is also a permanent display, the Ellen Rose-Fieldhouse Collection, mainly focusing on local history. The Parish of Kirkby Ireleth receives particular attention, and there is an interesting section on the Burlington Slate Quarries.

Going through the doors and into the main gallery, you will see a model of Barrow village as it might have appeared in 1845 just before its massive industrial expansion, the remains of which can be seen all over the town. To the left are display cases relating to early domestic life and agriculture: the Dutch oven was used in front of an open fire, its metal hood reflecting the heat into a 'Bottle Jack', a clockwork device that rotated the meat to distribute the heat evenly.

Items from farm and field include a peat spade and push plough (for use on marginal land), and some vicious spring-traps for all manner of beasts including humans! An interesting and informative display traces the development of lighting in rural areas from the early days of rush-lights (called nippers), to combined rush-lights and candles, and then to oil lamps.

However the real stars of the museum are undoubtedly the model ships. Built as maker's models by the shipyards, they were also used as marketing aids to sell the real thing. They are superb examples of the model-maker's art and make a journey to the Furness Museum worthwhile in their own right. Some names that stand out are the 11,000 ton HMS *Amphitrite* (1900), and HMS *Erin*, built as a battleship for the Turkish Navy and taken over by the Royal Navy in 1914.

There are merchant vessels too, such as MV *Moveria* (1927), the first diesel-engined vessel built with a fuel pressure injection system. There are also some speculative models like the Atlantic liner, never actually built but presumably used to tempt the shipping magnates.

The story of all these ships is inextricably linked with Barrow's history. The Furness Railway opened in the mid-nineteenth century, and within 30 years Barrow had the largest Bessemer steelworks in the world. By 1881, the Barrow yards could build ships like the *City of Rome,* a popular passenger liner.

History of a very different kind is displayed in the archaeology section. There are flints from Walney Island dating back 5,000 years, when the coast provided the main Stone Age settlement area. Methods of flint production are explained, as is the manufacture of the superb polished Lakeland stone axes. Prehistoric pottery is represented by a Bronze Age burial urn and some interesting items from Roosecote – an incense cup and a tiny food vessel.

You may have noticed that the museum is located in Ramsden Square; Sir James Ramsden was a leading figure in the development of the town and an active member of the Royal Barrow Yacht Club. Not surprisingly he had a fine steam yacht, *Aries*, built in 1875. Later wrecked off Holyhead, she was succeeded by *Aries II* in 1881. There is a builder's model of *Aries II* here, as well as photographs of her luxurious interior, presumably taken before she became an armed yacht during the First World War. (She was sunk by a mine in 1915.)

A very different method of transport is illustrated by a selection of old bicycles. This includes an 1870 Boneshaker, a rich man's toy and definitely not recommended for long journeys! The Penny Farthing was a more practical machine despite its strange appearance, but by far the most advanced bike on display is the Safety Bicycle of 1900 – safe, comfortable and cheaper to use than a horse or motorcar. It featured chain drive, rod brakes and, what joy, pneumatic tyres! If all this exertion proved too much you could always retire to the comfort of the bath chair – the museum has one of those too.

The Dock

This is a new museum development which at the time of writing was nearing completion. To find out details of its facilities and opening hours telephone (0229) 870871 or contact your local Tourist Information Centre.

If examining superbly constructed models inspires you to learn more about the shipbuilding history of the town, then you are likely to be interested in this major new museum development. Following current trends, the Dock will be much more than 'just a museum'. When complete the site will possess picnic areas, a pub restaurant, a cafeteria and a film theatre.

The unique building is actually set into a Victorian ship repair dock located down by the Walney Channel near the shipbuilding yards. The old dock has been divided up by a massive dam into 'wet' and 'dry' halves. The dry half is covered by a majestic glass

and steel structure on three floors. You enter through a visitor orientation centre on the dockside which will house the shop, cafeteria, theatre and a temporary exhibition gallery. Though the museum is not yet complete, I can perhaps give you a flavour of what you can expect to find.

Seafaring and boatbuilding have been at the heart of the Barrow community for many generations. From 1870 onwards, Barrow shipyard workers were at the forefront of the industry. The Barrow yards often led new advances in technology, and the town's products have ranged from elegant steam yachts to cargo vessels, from battleships to the deadly nuclear-powered submarines of today. In recent years Barrow yards have produced HMS *Invincible* which saw action in the Falklands and the P&O liner *Oriana,* the largest liner ever constructed in England.

The Dock Museum will feature the latest technology in order to surround you with the sights and sounds of ship construction. Displays will include the full-size stern of a passenger liner complete with propellers, a street scene from Barrow in its heyday, and a reconstructed shipyard drawing office where you will be able to use computers to design your own ship. If all this high-tech heritage proves too much you can always retreat outside to view the real vessels being restored.

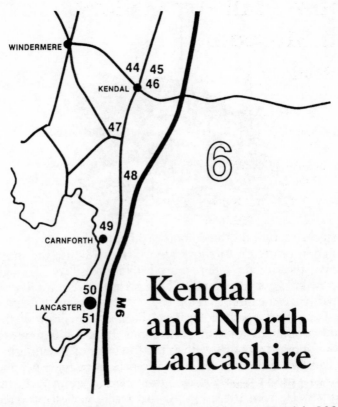

Kendal and North Lancashire

44 Abbot Hall Art Gallery and Museum, Kendal *139*
45 Museum of Lakeland Life and Industry, Kendal *142*
46 Kendal Museum of Archaeology and Natural History *145*
47 Levens Hall Steam Collection *148*
48 Heron Corn Mill, Beetham *150*
49 Steamtown Railway Museum, Carnforth *152*
50 Lancaster City Museum *155*
51 Lancaster Maritime Museum *156*

Abbot Hall Art Gallery and Museum
Kendal

Open All year *Admission charge*

Hours May–October: Monday–Saturday, 10.30–5.00; Sunday, 2.00–5.00

November–April: Monday–Friday, 10.30–5.00; Saturday and Sunday, 2.00–5.00

Address Abbot Hall, Kirkland, Kendal, Cumbria LA9 5AL

Telephone (0539) 722464

Suitability for children 10 years and above.

Refreshments There is plenty of choice nearby in the town centre.

Interest Fine art, furniture, craft and sculpture.

How to get there Abbot Hall is off Kirkland, near Kendal Parish Church, towards the south of the town. Take Junctions 36 or 37 off the M6. There is parking at the museum. The railway station is in Station Road, about 20 minutes walk away. The bus station is in Blackhall Road, about 15 minutes walk away.

Other attractions nearby Museum of Lakeland Life and Industry (p. 142), Brewery Arts Centre, and Kendal Museum of Archaeology and Natural History (p. 145) where the famous Wainwright was honorary curator for many years.

This is Cumbria's leading art gallery. Set in the relatively peaceful surroundings of a public park, the Hall dates back to 1759. In times past a number of notable families lived here but the building fell into disrepair in the 1950s. Strong local support for a renovation scheme eventually led to the Hall being opened as an art gallery by Princess Margaret in 1962. Since that time the Lake District Art Gallery and Museum Trust have worked hard to make Abbot Hall and its collections a centre of excellence

139

for fine art in Cumbria.

The building is divided into two main areas. The ground floor is devoted to period room settings furnished with fine regional furniture and works of art of national importance. Upstairs contemporary art galleries display works by some of Britain's foremost artists, such as Elizabeth Frink and Barbara Hepworth. There is also a temporary exhibition gallery where a lively and challenging programme of exhibitions provides something new virtually each month.

On entering the visitor walks first into the hallway of the old house. On the left is the museum shop and in front is a view of the riverside gardens and bowling green. The hallway contains some remarkable paintings and decorative features. The large oil painting *Belle Isle in a Storm* by Philip de Loutherbourg (1785) shows Lake Windermere in a storm that the Atlantic would be proud of. Whilst the pillars and pilasters of the hallway are original, the floor is made of new fossil-rich polished limestone from three local quarries at Orton Scar. To the left of the hallway is the breakfast room, panelled in painted wood and hung with paintings by such artists as John Constable.

Beyond this room is the former library which contains one of my favourite paintings, *Devoke Water* by William Blacklock (1853). You can almost smell the fresh mountain air! Also to be seen here is a collection of watercolours and other memorabilia belonging to John Ruskin, the Victorian philosopher and aesthete.

To the right of the hallway is the drawing room with its moulded plaster panels and richly decorated window frames. This room contains what at first sight might be mistaken for an eighteenth-century pool table. In fact it is a Trou Madame table built by Gillows and Taylor in 1773. The game was a more sophisticated version of shove ha'penny.

In the dining room beyond can be seen a large and impressive painting of the Gower family by George Romney done in about 1776. This painting is regarded as Romney's masterpiece and was purchased with help from many generous donors.

Abbot Hall is currently undergoing substantial improvement

and enlargement. The roof you will see has only very recently been added and replaces a flat roof which the building was given after its first renovation in 1950. Upstairs will be two new galleries, one devoted to the large collection of contemporary art and the other to a changing display of views of Lakeland. The art gallery also runs a very good craft shop located at the entrance to the Farming Gallery by the car park.

Abbot Hall

Abbot Hall is a place to spend time looking at how artists have interpreted Lakeland through the ages, to view paintings and furniture of a style and quality rarely seen, and to learn a little about Lake District 'high life' over the last 300 years. If the younger members of the family are reluctant to absorb all this culture then divide the party and send them to the Museum of Lakeland Life and Industry just across the courtyard.

Museum of Lakeland Life and Industry
Kendal

Open All year *Admission charge*

Hours May–October: Monday–Saturday, 10.30–5.00; Sunday, 2.00–5.00

November–April: Monday–Friday, 10.30–5.00; Saturday and Sunday, 2.00–5.00

Address Abbot Hall, Kirkland, Kendal, Cumbria LA9 5AL

Telephone (0539) 722464

Suitability for children All ages.

Refreshments Available nearby in the town centre.

Interest Industrial, local and literary history.

How to get there Leave the M6 at Junctions 36 or 37 to Kendal. The museum is located in Kirkland towards the south end of town. Parking is available on site. Kendal railway station is about 20 minutes walk away; the bus station about 15 minutes.

Other attractions nearby Abbot Hall (p. 139), Kendal Museum of Archaeology and Natural History (p. 145), and the Brewery Arts Centre. Kendal Castle ruins are also worth a visit, as is the ever-popular K's shoe factory shop.

This fascinating museum is housed in the eighteenth-century stable block belonging to Abbot Hall. It was opened in 1971, inspired by local concern that the traditional Lakeland lifestyle was beginning to disappear under the weight of increasing numbers of tourists. The old ways have now almost disappeared, but this museum takes you back in time.

The entrance is through the small shop which sits in the middle of the old gateway to Abbot Hall, and the first display depicts some aggressive-looking men, participants in that well-known local sport, Cumberland wrestling. The trophies and prizes they won over the years are shown here, as are many photographs of them resplendent in their colourful embroidered shorts.

Wicker pram (courtesy of Lake District Museum and Art Gallery Trust)

A more sedate aspect of Lakeland life is illustrated by the next display which covers the local wool trade and includes a Victorian loom. A large colourful painting depicts many aspects of the medieval trade and you can spend some time just examining the detail, and reflecting on the influence the industry has had on local life. This influence continues to the present day. Surnames such as Webster, Dyer, Fuller and Walker for example, all owe their origins to the wool industry, and some common expressions are derived from the wool trade too. To be 'on tenterhooks' is one, and the coat of arms for Kendal has the motto 'Pannus mihi panis' – 'Wool is my bread'.

Next you will find a reconstructed room of the late eighteenth or early nineteenth century filled with regional furniture characteristic of the Westmorland tradition. It's like walking uninvited into somebody's private house – you can feel quite out of place at first. Continuing upstairs you will come across an effective recreation of a farmhouse kitchen or 'firehouse' of the mid-eighteenth century, complete with bread and fruit. The child's highchair is apparently a fairly restrained example of the Westmorland furniture style but it still looks very cumbersome and distinctly uncomfortable.

There are more room reconstructions and displays of costume and jewellery upstairs. Industry in the Lakes is well represented by very realistic reconstructed workshops including those of a blacksmith, a clog-maker, a boot-maker, and a painter. The painter's door is literally inches thick with paint flicked from his brushes. The particularly Cumbrian industry of bobbin-making is featured with a bobbin lathe that turned at around 6,000 rpm and could produce 20 reels a minute, if the operator was skilled enough. An imaginative rebuild of a section of an iron mine gives children the illusion of exploring deep underground; there are even safety helmets to put on before you enter!

Elsewhere on this upper floor are a toy gallery, complete with some amazingly realistic dolls, and a room devoted to Arthur Ransome, the creator of the *Swallows and Amazons* children's books. Here you can read some of his letters and view his personal possessions in a room that is the focus for a rapidly expanding Arthur Ransome Society (details from the museum staff).

Our tour ends with a late nineteenth-century street scene featuring a Marks Penny Bazaar (the forerunner of the modern Marks and Spencer). Close by there is a brightly painted fire engine from Runcorn, though I must confess I didn't discover its connection with Kendal.

Nowadays only ghosts inhabit this world of steam engines, bobbin lathes and furniture-makers' workshops. You can, however, call up some of those spirits in this wonderful museum, and enjoy immersing yourself in another age.

Museum of Archaeology and Natural History
Kendal

Open All year *Admission charge*

Hours April–October: Monday–Saturday, 10.30–5.00; Sunday, 2.00–5.00

November–March: Monday–Friday, 10.30–5.00; Saturday and Sunday, 2.00–5.00

Address Station Road, Kendal, Cumbria LA9 6BT

Telephone (0539) 721374

Suitability for children All ages.

Interest Natural history, local history and world wildlife.

How to get there The museum is out of the town centre on the east side, close to the railway station (on the Windermere line). Parking is available on site. There are good bus connections to Kendal; the bus station is in Blackhall Road about five minutes walk away.

Other attractions nearby Abbot Hall (p. 139), Museum of Lakeland Life and Industry (p. 142) and the Brewery Arts Centre.

This award-winning museum began life as the private collection of a Mr Todhunter, who first set up his exhibition of curiosities in 1796. In the 1830s the collection passed into the hands of the Kendal Literary and Scientific Society. Then in 1913 the museum moved to the present building, a former wool ware-house, and it was eventually taken over by the local Council in 1974.

On entering you first see the busts of some local worthies who contributed to the establishment of the early museum. There are also some posters and handbills from the early days. Beyond this is the museum shop.

As you enter the gallery to your right, a rather alarming Neolithic man is poised above you chipping away at a rough-hewn stone axe. He's obviously working hard since his face is distinctly purple! A range of Neolithic artefacts is displayed below him: flints; polished stone axes; and bronze work.

Further into the gallery are some Roman remains from the forts at Watercrook, Waterhead and Low Borrow Bridge. There are the usual fragments of Samian ware (bright red-gloss pottery, no doubt a status symbol for aspiring Roman commanders), and memorial stones dedicated to various Roman gods and set up by friends of soldiers killed in action.

Soldiers of the imagination are replaced by brightly painted soldier figurines, dressed in medieval armour, in an interesting display located beyond the Roman cases. George Pallant Sideaway made these models because of his frustration at seeing inaccurate costumes used in films and on TV. He set about making these accurate replicas to help film-makers achieve greater authenticity. There are also medieval coins and pottery here, as well as more recent exhibits on Westmorland life. (Cumbria was once two counties: Westmorland and Cumberland – and a bit of Lancashire – and a fierce tribal rivalry still exists between the old shires.) Glorious costumes and evil instruments of torture, such as thumbscrews and waist irons, share the stage for the last few centuries. Here we also find a ship's bell, from HMS *Kendal*, a First World War mine-sweeper.

Perhaps the most entertaining item on the ground floor is the reconstruction of a curator's office and displays from 20 years ago (some museums don't need reconstructions!). The displays have been laid out with handwritten labels, and widely differing objects snuggle up to each other in the same cases: a game of Nine Men's Morris, bone skates and a turtle from Fiji, in one. There's a huge array of copper coins and, hidden by a protective green cloth, some birds' eggs and a herbarium (dried flowers).

Closer investigation in this section will reveal that A. Wainwright, of the famous hand-drawn walking guides to the Lakes, was once an honorary curator. (The museum stores are full of objects with labels written in his meticulous accountant's hand.) There are Egyptian artefacts here too: scarabs; fertility figurines; and beadwork.

The real treasure house is upstairs. Here the Lake District Natural History Gallery invites you to discover the inner secrets of this unique landscape. Stunning dioramas create windows that allow you to look into various natural habitats; my favourites are the Kendal Garden and the Windermere Sub-Surface. The complex geology of the area is well illustrated, from 520 million years ago through to more recent times. There are plenty of fossils for children to discover and there's a 'feely table' full of objects which you handle in order to guess their origins.

Golden Eagle (courtesy of South Lakeland Borough Council)

Back downstairs and turning right you enter a gallery which contains an amazing collection of stuffed animals and birds from all over the world. How did they get to Kendal? They are the collection of Colonel C. Harrison, a hunter of the old school, from a time when the environment was regarded as a place stocked with moving targets for eager sportsmen. One hopes that period in our history is now over, but the World Wildlife Gallery does give us the opportunity to gaze in wonder at the rich variety of life on the planet. Where else would you see a polar bear and a duck-billed platypus in the same room?

Levens Hall
Steam Collection
Levens

Open Easter–September *Admission charge*

Hours 11.00–5.00, Sunday–Thursday

Address Levens Hall, Kendal, Cumbria LA8 0PB

Telephone (05395) 60321

Suitability for children All ages.

Refreshments There are tea rooms on site.

Interest Steam engines and historic houses.

How to get there Levens Hall is located on the A6, south of Kendal, and there is parking on site. The nearest railway stations are at Oxenholme and Carnforth. There are buses from Carnforth and Milnthorpe.

Other attractions nearby Heron Corn Mill (p. 150), Abbot Hall Art Gallery and Museum (p. 139) and Sizergh Castle (owned by the National Trust).

Levens Hall, the largest Elizabethan house in Cumbria, dates back to the late sixteenth and early seventeenth centuries. The building (still privately owned) is open to the public, as are the spectacular gardens, which include some very fine examples of topiary (tree sculpture).

The adjacent outbuildings house the Levens Hall Steam Collection, gathered by a former owner of the house. The collection mainly consists of scale models of stationary steam engines (of the type used in mills, mines and numerous workshops during the nineteenth century).

The first room you enter contains some static exhibits, such as the twin cylinder compound marine engine, typical of the type used in the steam launches which once plied the nearby lakes. There is also the Levens Hall fire engine, a rather grand title for such a small – but no doubt efficient – pump.

Leaving this room, you are drawn by the smell of steam and hot oil into the main gallery, where all the working models are quietly rotating and leaking steam. (They have an automatic lubrication system which allows them to run for long periods without attention.) To the left is a large revolving waterwheel, which came from a Cornish tin mine and illustrates the source of energy used for pumping in mines before the age of steam. At first glance, all the other occupants of the room appear to be steam engines, but there are a few interlopers! Off to one side are some hot air engines, such as the Robinson patent of 1900 which was used for driving shop window displays and generators in houses.

Moving around the room you will soon spot the large brass plate on the wall. This comes from the Great Western Railway locomotive *Levens Hall*, designed by C.B. Collett, which once ran in south-west England. Just below it is a delightful six-pillar single-cylinder condensing rotative beam engine from about 1920. And in the fireplace is an instrument maker's model of a single-cylinder Watt-Type condensing rotative beam engine of around 1820, designed for instructional use. There are also two traction engines. *Little Gem* is a scale model which is steamed regularly to provide rides for children, and in a nearby shed is a full-sized, powerful-looking, traction engine called *Bertha*.

Heron Corn Mill
Beetham

Open Easter–September (school parties taken in October if pre-booked), *Admission charge*

Hours 11.00–5.00, Tuesday–Sunday and Bank Holidays

Address The Administrator, Heron Corn Mill, c/o Henry Cooke Ltd, Waterhouse Mills, Beetham, Milnthorpe, Cumbria LA7 7AR

Telephone (0524) 734858

Suitability for children All ages.

Refreshments A small museum café is planned for 1991.

Interest Technology and local history.

How to get there The mill is signposted off the old A6 at Beetham, south of Milnthorpe. The nearest railway station is at Carnforth, and there are buses from Carnforth and Kendal.

Other attractions nearby Levens Hall Steam Collection (p. 148) and Steamtown (p. 152).

Heron Corn Mill dates back as early as 1096. Since then it has had a varied history, operating commercially until 1955. In 1973 Henry Cooke Ltd, the paper-makers in the Waterhouse Mills over the river, leased the corn mill to the newly formed Beetham Trust.

The present building is approximately 260 years old and contains a working example of a Louder Mill (which is nothing to do with noise, but describes the machinery used!). In the nearby barn is a display on the history of paper-making, opened in 1988 to commemorate 500 years of British paper-making.

Away from the barn and down towards the River Bela lies the mill itself. You enter at ground level and to your right is the drying kiln where fresh corn was dried prior to grinding. The floor is made up of perforated baked clay tiles and the heat came from a fireplace in the basement. The main room is almost filled by the massive timber 'hurst frame' supporting the grinding stones and their gearing. The various bits of machinery possess wonderful names – damazel, Great Spur Wheel, wallower, jog scry. When set in motion by the flow of water on to the main waterwheel, you can watch corn being ground by the four revolving sets of millstones, each pair set with such precision that they are just millimetres apart.

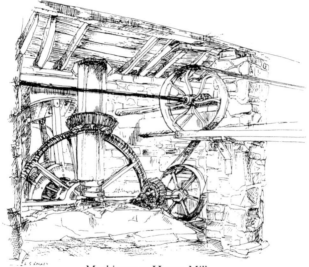

Machinery at Heron Mill

If you can tear yourself away from the glass observation window set above the waterwheel you can go downstairs to see it close to. For the technically minded it is a 14-foot-high breast-shot wheel. By a system of well-greased gears the power is transmitted up to the floor above by the huge wallower shaft. Above your head are other subsidiary line shafts and pulleys, all in continuous motion.

Until the introduction of electricity and steam power the River Bela had a long history as a source of energy. Heron Corn Mill epitomises the use of that renewable resource, taking its requirements without pollution. As an example of 'alternative' technology it is as valid today as it was in its heyday.

Steamtown
Railway Museum
Carnforth

Open All year *Admission charge*

Hours Easter–October: 9.00–5.00 every day
November–March: 10.00–4.00 except Christmas

Address Steamtown, Warton Road, Carnforth, Lancashire
LA5 9HX

Telephone (0524) 732100

Suitability for children All ages but keep an eye on young
children – this is a working rail depot.

Refreshments Food and drink are available in a converted railway
carriage on site.

Interest Steam engines, railways and nostalgia.

How to get there Take the A6 to Carnforth. Steamtown is
signposted from the town centre and is located beyond the main
railway station, which is just a short walk away. There is parking on
site.

Other attractions nearby Lancaster City and Maritime Museums
(p. 155), Levens Hall Steam Collection (p. 148).

Steamtown is located in a former BR locomotive depot which
closed in 1969. In the old days Carnforth was served by three
railway companies: the Furness Railway, the London and North-
Western Railway and the Midland Railway, each having their
own locomotive shed. In 1923 the three companies were amalgamated into the London Midland and Scottish Railway and this
company soon realised the savings it could make in locomotive
servicing. A 'cafeteria' system was devised for coaling, watering
and fire cleaning; and the old separate engine sheds at places
such as Carnforth were combined into one massive depot. The

depot we see today was in fact built by Italian prisoners of war in 1942.

Steamtown is not a static museum, for the depot is the home of many active engines used on main-line excursions all over the country, and you can often see steam and diesel locomotives actually running. At the far end of the site you will find the terminus of the miniature railway that runs the length of the depot – this is an excellent way of getting from one end to the other. There are three steam engines used on this line and they make an interesting comparison with their giant counterparts elsewhere.

It is difficult to predict which of the main-line steam locomotives will be in the depot when you visit. The star attractions are undoubtedly the *Flying Scotsman*, the LNER express locomotive, unmistakable in its lime green livery; and *Sir Nigel Gresley*, named after the famous locomotive designer, and a sister to *Mallard* which possesses the 124 mph world speed record for a steam locomotive.

There are other engines here too, less spectacular perhaps than the stylish expresses, but all possessing their own personalities. The elderly Lancashire and Yorkshire 0–6–0, No. 1122, built in 1896, demonstrates the exposed conditions the early enginemen had to work in. Away from the glory of the main line were the many branch and industrial lines, and here the small but powerful industrial locos held sway. There are many representatives of the breed here but perhaps the most attractive is *Lindsay*. Built in 1887, she was formerly used by the Wigan Coal and Iron Company and rescued from the scrapyard in 1976. In the large engine sheds you will see a number of engines in bits during restoration. The sheer size of some of the components is awe-inspiring.

Elsewhere on the site you will find the museum exhibition. This contains some fascinating relics of the railway era, as well as a rather good reconstruction of an old ticket office. The walls of the main room are covered in old signs from various railway companies, and the display cases contain some real curiosities: silver and ceramic mementos from the LNWR and Midland railways (including a Midland Railway whisky flask), and some Furness Railway Coupling Contest cups – the mind boggles!

The elegance of Pullman travel is recalled with numerous items of publicity material and timetables. One display is devoted to the *Flying Scotsman* and her history, including some souvenirs from her trips to America and Australia. There are some intriguing headboards on the walls, with famous names such as *The Fair Maid, The White Rose, The Half Century Limited* and, more mundanely, *The Whitehaven to Huddersfield TPO* (travelling post office). There are also items of instruction for trainee enginemen, such as a wooden model of valve gear and the curious 'Midland Railway Colour Blindness Testing Kit' – important if you were to read signals correctly!

At the south end of the miniature railway line, is 'Collectors' Corner', a shop selling all kinds of railway memorabilia, from badges to lamps. At the north end of the line, in a converted rail wagon, is a '00' scale model railway which includes a working mountain line. To satisfy any desperate urge to start modelling there is a well-stocked model shop next door.

You can almost sense the ghosts of the old enginemen as you wander round a place like Steamtown – their pride and skill shines through even today. If you get a chance to stand on the footplate of an express locomotive whilst you are there it is not difficult to understand why every young boy once wanted to be an engine-driver.

City Museum and Maritime Museum

Lancaster

Open All year *Admission free*

Hours 10.00–5.00, Monday–Saturday

Address City Museum, Market Square, Lancaster LA1 1HT
Maritime Museum, Custom House, St George's Quay, Lancaster
LA1 1RB

Telephone (0524) 64637 for both museums

Suitability for children All ages.

Refreshments The Maritime Museum has a good café; otherwise
there's a wide choice in the city centre.

Interest Local and maritime history.

How to get there Lancaster is on the main West Coast rail line
from London to Glasgow. The railway station is about 10 minutes
walk away from the City Museum; the bus station is in Cable Street,
also about 10 minutes walk away. There is plenty of parking in multi-
storey and pay and display car-parks nearby.

Other attractions nearby Steamtown Railway Museum (p. 152)
and Morecambe Bay and Heysham Nuclear Power Station.

The City Museum

The City Museum is located in the old Town Hall, built between
1781 and 1783 by a Major Jarrott and Thomas Harrison. There
are two floors of displays, with two temporary exhibition galleries
downstairs, and the main galleries upstairs.

At the foot of the main staircase stands a majestic Roman
milestone from Artle Beck, dating from the time of Emperor
Hadrian, around AD 120. The staircase itself is lined with some
fine examples from the museum's collection of works of art,

155

many showing local views and the changing face of the city over the centuries. At the top of the stairs you face a corridor gallery with a small shop, and wall cases focusing on local history: the Scotforth and Burton Pottery, for example; some colourful (and painful-looking) truncheons from the local constabulary; and examples of ironwork from the local foundries.

Off to the right is a room devoted to archaeology and more local history. There are some notable curiosities, such as the Celtic stone head found in the rubble of a demolished chimney breast in a local house, or the various charms against witchcraft, particularly the rattle.

Lancaster was traditionally a centre of furniture production, and the firm of Gillows made many fine mahogany pieces, some of which are on display here. (You'll see other examples up at Abbot Hall in Kendal, p. 139). Something else you can't fail to notice in this gallery are the Roman sculpted stone heads from the Burrow Mausoleum Group, found during the excavation of the canal, near Burrow Heights.

The next room is given over to displays of military history, featuring the 4th Regiment of Foot and The King's Own Royal Border Regiment (Lancaster). It's a rather old-fashioned display of uniforms and medals, soon to be changed and improved, but it has an interesting section on regimental sport.

The Maritime Museum

Lancaster Maritime Museum is to be found in the restored Customs House (dating back to 1764) on St George's Quay. It is flanked by a range of late eighteenth-century quayside buildings, all constructed at a time of flourishing trade with the West Indies, North America and Europe. A recent extension into the adjoining warehouse has enlarged the display area and the whole museum contains many fascinating maritime exhibits.

As you enter the building you are greeted by a rather immodest but colourful figurehead, and some superb models of sailing ships. There was also, when I visited, an interactive computer game with which you could test your knowledge of ships and the sea. The various rooms on the rest of this floor are given over to trade: imports, such as sugar from the West Indies; and exports, such as felt hats and silk. Note also the Gillows furniture again, made from wood imported from the Caribbean.

Moving from the hall and down some spiral steps (there is also a lift), you come to an area featuring the local fishing industry. There's a complete original Whammel boat, the *Hannah*, built in 1910, and a small aquarium containing some live examples of marine life from Morecambe Bay. All aspects of fishing are well covered, and shrimping is described in detail, with a reconstruction of a shrimper's kitchen (when I was there even the smell was authentic). Shrimps are caught at sea in 'Nobbies' (single-masted vessels with two crew) which have a boiler to process the catch at sea. The victims of this industry are represented by some rather sad-looking examples of a preserved shrimp and prawn.

Passing through this gallery and into the shop (well stocked with things maritime, books and souvenirs), you can walk (or take the lift) to the top floor of the adjoining warehouse. Once there you find a welcoming tea shop and some modern displays about Morecambe Bay. Here you can walk through an imaginatively laid out section about a gas rig (CPC1, 26 miles west of Blackpool), and look at a feature on the Heysham nuclear power station and its effect on the environment. Among other interesting facts, the station requires 50 million gallons of sea water an hour for cooling. That's the equivalent of two Olympic swimming pools a minute!

In an adjoining gallery are very effective reconstructions of two local forms of transport, both with dramatised audio commentaries. The first is of a packet boat from the Lancaster Canal. Before the coming of the railways these vessels plied the waterway between Kendal and Preston, a distance of about 30 miles, in three hours. They were pulled at a gallop by pairs of horses and were equivalent to today's express coaches (though the canal locks presumably slowed them down a bit). Also in this gallery is a horse-drawn coach from Morecambe Bay which used to travel from Ulverston to Lancaster at low tide, across

157

the treacherous sands of the Bay. There is a display on the guides whose job it was to lead travellers across the ever-shifting sands. Two guides are still employed today.

The Maritime Museum is an excellent example of good museum display and interpretation. Let us hope the City Museum will in time have the same resources devoted to it. Elsewhere in the city are to be found the Judges' Lodgings at the head of Church Street (now a museum housing yet more Gillow furniture); a Museum of Childhood including the Barry Elder Collection of Dolls; and the Cottage Museum on Castle Hill, which displays period rooms of about 1825, and is furnished as a worker's cottage.

Reconstruction of Morecambe Bay fishing family's cottage

List of Museums by Subject Heading

Archaeology

Armitt Library Ambleside *83*
Birdoswald Roman Fort,
    Brampton *18*
Carlisle Cathedral Treasury *27*
Furness Museum, Barrow *134*
Guildhall, Carlisle *30*
Kendal Museum of Archaeology and
    Natural History *145*
Keswick Museum and Art Gallery *71*
Lancaster City Museum *155*
Millom Folk Museum *125*
Penrith Town Museum *104*
Roman Army Museum,
    Greenhead *15*
Ruskin Museum, Coniston *88*
Senhouse Roman Army Museum,
    Maryport *38*
Tullie House, Carlisle *32*
Whitehaven Museum *53*

Art

Abbot Hall, Kendal *139*
Armitt Library, Ambleside *83*
Beatrix Potter Gallery,
    Hawkshead *85*
Brantwood, Coniston *94*
Carlisle Cathedral Treasury *27*
Keswick Museum and Art Gallery *71*
Lancaster City Museum *155*
Ruskin Museum, Coniston *88*
Tullie House, Carlisle *32*
Wetheriggs Country Pottery *111*
Whitehaven Museum *53*
Wordsworth Museum and Dove
    Cottage, Grasmere *77*

Children's Entertainment, Toys and Models

Beatrix Potter Gallery,
    Hawkshead *85*
Cars of the Stars, Keswick *74*
Cumberland Pencil Museum,
    Keswick *68*
Cumberland Toy and Model
    Museum, Cockermouth *44*
Lakeland Motor Museum, Holker
    Hall *130*
Lakeside and Haverthwaite
    Railway *123*
Laurel and Hardy Museum,
    Ulverston *128*
Levens Hall Steam Collection *148*
Museum of Lakeland Life and
    Industry, Kendal *142*
Penrith Steam Museum *107*
Ravenglass and Eskdale Railway
    Museum *61*
Roman Army Museum,
    Greenhead *15*
Sellafield Visitor Centre *56*
Solway Aviation Museum, Carlisle
    Airport *21*
Steamtown Railway Museum,
    Carnforth *152*
Tullie House, Carlisle *32*
Windermere Steamboat Museum *91*

Geology

Brantwood, Coniston *94*
Caldbeck Mining Museum *35*
Kendal Museum of Archaeology and
    Natural History *145*
Keswick Museum and Art Gallery *71*
Penrith Town Museum *104*
Ruskin Museum, Coniston *88*
Whitehaven Museum *53*

Industrial and Agricultural History

Caldbeck Mining Museum *35*
Cumberland Pencil Museum,
    Keswick *68*
Dalemain, Penrith *114*
Dyke Nook Farm, Appleby *117*
Eskdale Corn Mill, Boot *58*

Heron Corn Mill, Beetham *150*
Killhope Wheel, Stanhope *98*
Millom Folk Museum *125*
Muncaster Mill, Ravenglass *63*
Museum of Lakeland Life and
  Industry, Kendal *142*
Penrith Steam Museum *107*
Sellafield Visitor Centre *56*
Stott Park Bobbin Mill,
  Finsthwaite *121*
Wetheriggs Country Pottery,
  Penrith *111*
Whitehaven Museum *53*
Wythop Mill, Embleton *47*

Literary History

Armitt Library Ambleside *83*
Beatrix Potter Gallery,
  Hawkshead *85*
Brantwood, Coniston *94*
Keswick Museum and Art Gallery *71*
Millom Folk Museum *125*
Museum of Lakeland Life and
  Industry, Kendal *142*
Ruskin Museum, Coniston *88*
Rydal Mount, Ambleside *80*
Wordsworth Museum and Dove
  Cottage, Grasmere *77*

Military History (*all Periods*)

Birdoswald Roman Fort,
  Brampton *18*
Border Regiment Museum,
  Carlisle *24*
Dalemain, Penrith *114*
Lancaster City Museum *155*
Roman Army Museum,
  Greenhead *15*
Senhouse Roman Army Museum,
  Maryport *38*
Solway Aviation Museum, Carlisle
  Airport *21*

Natural History

Dalemain, Penrith *114*

Kendal Museum of Archaeology and
  Natural History *145*
Keswick Museum and Art Gallery *71*
Tullie House, Carlisle *32*

Social History

Abbot Hall, Kendal *139*
Cumberland Toy and Model
  Museum, Cockermouth *44*
Cumbria Police Museum,
  Penrith *101*
Furness Museum, Barrow *134*
Guildhall, Carlisle *30*
Helena Thompson Museum,
  Workington *50*
Kendal Museum of Archaeology and
  Natural History *145*
Keswick Museum and Art Gallery *71*
Lancaster City Museum *155*
Laurel and Hardy Museum,
  Ulverston *128*
Millom Folk Museum *125*
Museum of Lakeland Life and
  Industry, Kendal *142*
Penrith Town Museum *104*
Tullie House, Carlisle *32*
Whitehaven Museum *53*

Transport

Cars of the Stars, Keswick *74*
The Dock, Barrow *136*
Lakeland Motor Museum, Holker
  Hall *130*
Lakeside and Haverthwaite
  Railway *123*
Lancaster Maritime Museum *156*
Maryport Maritime Museum *41*
Penrith Steam Museum *107*
Ravenglass and Eskdale Railway
  Museum *61*
Solway Aviation Museum, Carlisle
  Airport *21*
Steamtown Railway Museum,
  Carnforth *152*
Windermere Steamboat Museum *91*